Scraping the Web: Python in Action and Beyond

A Comprehensive Guide to Web Scraping and Automation

By: Ali Jafari

About the Author

Ali Jafari is a seasoned data analyst and web developer with extensive experience in building web scrapers and automating workflows. Through his professional journey, he has tackled diverse challenges in data extraction and analysis, helping businesses gain actionable insights from web data. This book reflects his commitment to sharing knowledge and empowering others to harness the power of Python for web scraping and automation.

Acknowledgments

Special thanks to the vibrant Python and open-source communities whose tools and contributions make web scraping accessible to all.

This comprehensive guide provides a detailed overview of web scraping and automation using Python, covering everything from basic concepts to advanced techniques and real-world applications. Let me know if you need further assistance!

Alijafarixcs@gmail.com

https://github.com/alijafarixcs/

Table of Contents

Scraping the Web: Python in Action and Beyond 1

About the Author 2

Acknowledgments 2

    Who This Book is For 9

    What You Will Learn 9

Chapter 1: Python Basics for Web Scraping 10

    Introduction 10

    Why Python Is Good for Industry 11

    Chapter 1.0.1: Data Types 11

        1.0.1.1 Basic Data Types 11

        1.0.1.2 Complex Data Types 12

        1.0.1.3 Type Conversion 13

    Chapter 1.0.2: Control Flow 13

        1.0.2.1 Conditional Statements 13

        1.0.2.2 Loops 14

        1.0.2.3 Break and Continue 14

        1.0.2.4 Nested Loops 14

        1.0.2.5 Exception Handling 14

    Chapter 1.0.3.: Mastering Object-Oriented Programming in Python 15

        1.0.3.1. Classes and Objects 15

        1.0.3.2. Encapsulation 15

        1.0.3.3. Inheritance 15

        1.0.3.4. Polymorphism 16

        1.0.3.5. Abstraction 16

    Conclusion 17

        Summary of OOP 17

Chapter 2: Introduction to Web Scraping 17

    2.1 What is Web Scraping? 17

    2.2 Key Use Cases 18

    2.3 Legal and Ethical Considerations 19

    2.4 Setting Up Your Environment 19

        2.4.1 Writing Python Code in Your IDE 19

        2.4.2 Understanding the Setup Commands 20

        Chapter Summary 26

Chapter 3: Understanding HTML and the DOM 26

    HTML Basics and Structure 26

The DOM: A Tree Representation of HTML 27
Using Browser Developer Tools 27
Key DOM Features 28
    Dynamic Content 28
    Selectors 28
    Practical Example: Extracting Data 29

Chapter 4: Python Basics for Web Scraping 32
4.1 Installing Necessary Libraries 33
4.2 Fundamentals of Python for Data Extraction 33
4.3 Writing Your First Scraper 34
Chapter Summary 36

Chapter 5: Using BeautifulSoup for Static Pages 37
5.1 Extracting Data from Static HTML 37
5.2 Navigating and Searching the DOM 37
5.3 Handling Common Challenges 38
Complete Example: Scraping Data with BeautifulSoup 39
    Chapter BS4 Poupular methods 40
    Explanation of Each Method and Property: 42
    Use Cases for These Methods: 42
    Chapter Summary 43

Chapter 6: Scraping Dynamic Websites with Selenium 43
6.1 Introduction to Selenium for Browser Automation 43
6.2 Handling JavaScript-Rendered Content 44
6.3 Interacting with Forms, Buttons, and Dropdowns 45
    Chapter Summary 46

Chapter 7: Advanced Web Scraping Techniques 47
7.1 Handling CAPTCHAs 47
7.2 Rotating User Agents and Proxies 48
7.3 Managing Sessions and Cookies 49
    Chapter Summary 50

Chapter 8: Data Cleaning and Storage 51
8.1 Cleaning Scraped Data 51
8.2 Storing Data in CSV, Excel, and Databases 52
8.3 Visualizing Data 53
    Chapter Summary 54

Chapter 9: Automating Tasks 54
9.1 Automating Repetitive Tasks 54

- Step 1: Setting Up Python 54
- Step 2: Writing the Web Scraping Script 55
- Step 3: Saving the Data to a File 55
- 9.2 Scheduling Scrapers 56
  - Using Cron Jobs: Setting Up Cron Jobs on Unix-Based Systems 56
  - Task Schedulers for Windows: Using Task Scheduler to Automate Script Execution 56
- 9.3 Sending Alerts and Notifications 57
  - Email Notifications: Sending Email Alerts Based on Scraped Data 57
- Chapter Summary 58

Chapter 10: Case Studies and Projects 58

- 10.1 Project 1: Building a Market Trend Scraper 58
  - Objective: 58
  - Tools and Techniques: 58
  - Python Code Example: 59
  - Explanation of Code: 59
- 10.2 Project 2: Automating Price Comparison for E-commerce 60
  - Objective: 60
  - Tools and Techniques: 60
  - Python Code Example: 60
  - Explanation of Code: 61
- 10.3 Project 3: Extracting Job Postings from Multiple Websites 61
  - Objective: 61
  - Tools and Techniques: 61
  - Python Code Example: 61
  - Explanation of Code: 62
- 10.4 Project 4: Social Media Sentiment Analysis with Web Scraping 62
  - Objective: 62
  - Tools and Techniques: 62
  - Python Code Example: 62
  - Explanation of Code: 63
- Chapter Summary 63

Chapter 11: Best Practices and Future Directions 65

- 11.1 Writing Efficient and Maintainable Code 65
- 11.2 Staying Within Ethical and Legal Boundaries 67
- 11.3 Future Trends in Web Scraping and Automation 68
- Chapter Summary 69

Chapter 12: The Road Ahead: A Vision for the Future 70
Setting Up ChromeDriver 70
Code Explanation 71
Additional Notes 71
Troubleshooting Common Issues 72
1. Imports 72
2. Class Definition - `StepstoneScrapper` 72
3. Constructor `__init__` Method 72
4. scrap_url Method 73
5. Quit WebDriver 74
6. Return Results 74
7. Main Execution Block 74
Summary of the Process: 75
Possible Improvements: 75
1. Import Statements 75
2. Adding Custom Library Path 76
3. Importing Custom Scraper 76
4. Instantiating the Scraper 76
5. Scraping Job Listings 77
6. Setting Pandas Display Options 77
7. Converting Data to DataFrame and Saving to CSV 77
Summary of the Process: 77
Possible Improvements: 78
Appendix A: Common Errors and Debugging Tips 78
Appendix B: Recommended Resources for Further Learning 81

Preface:

Web scraping and automation have become integral to various industries, especially for data analysts, developers, and businesses aiming to extract valuable insights from vast amounts of online data. In today's data-driven world, the role of data science, machine learning (ML), and artificial intelligence (AI) is growing exponentially, as they enable businesses to harness the power of data for decision-making and predictive modeling.

Web scraping refers to the process of extracting data from websites using automated scripts or software tools. By accessing publicly available information online, web scraping allows organizations to gather large datasets that are often used for research, market analysis, competitor tracking, and more. Automation, on the other hand, streamlines repetitive tasks and processes, increasing efficiency and reducing human error.

This book provides a comprehensive guide for mastering web scraping and automation using Python, a popular programming language for data analysis and automation tasks. It covers both the theoretical foundations, such as understanding HTML structure, web protocols, and data parsing techniques, and practical applications, including working with libraries like BeautifulSoup, Scrapy, and Selenium.

Data science plays a crucial role in turning raw data into actionable insights. By applying ML and AI techniques, data scientists can analyze scraped data, uncover patterns, and build predictive models. For example, scraping product data from e-commerce websites could lead to the development of recommendation systems, price comparison tools, or sales forecasting models.

Machine learning (ML) algorithms can be applied to the data collected from web scraping to detect trends, automate categorization, and predict future behavior. AI, especially in the form of natural language processing (NLP) and image recognition, can enhance web scraping by making it smarter, allowing for more sophisticated data extraction from unstructured sources like news articles or social media posts.

Effective data collection is a foundational step for any AI or ML project, as the quality and volume of data directly impact the performance of algorithms. With the right scraping tools and automation techniques, vast amounts of structured and unstructured data can be collected, cleaned, and fed into models for further analysis.

In essence, this book not only teaches the technical skills needed for web scraping and automation with Python but also explores how these tools empower data scientists, machine learning engineers, and businesses to extract and utilize online data for diverse purposes, from improving customer experiences to optimizing operational workflows.

Python plays a central role in the world of web scraping, automation, data science, and machine learning, making it a go-to programming language for professionals in these fields. Its simplicity, versatility, and robust ecosystem of libraries have contributed to its widespread adoption for tasks ranging from web scraping to advanced AI and ML applications.

For web scraping, Python's popularity is largely due to its rich selection of open-source libraries, such as BeautifulSoup, Scrapy, and Selenium, which provide powerful tools for parsing HTML, interacting with websites, and automating browsing tasks. These libraries make it easier for developers and data analysts to extract and process data from websites efficiently, regardless of the complexity or structure of the data.

In the broader context of data science and machine learning, Python is equally crucial. Libraries like Pandas, NumPy, and Matplotlib enable data scientists to clean, manipulate, and visualize large datasets. For machine learning and AI, Python's extensive ecosystem includes TensorFlow, Keras, PyTorch, and Scikit-learn, which simplify the development of predictive models and deep learning systems.

The open-source community plays an equally important role in the success and accessibility of Python-based tools. The open-source nature of Python allows developers worldwide to contribute to the improvement and expansion of libraries, ensuring they remain up-to-date and capable of addressing emerging challenges in web scraping, automation, data science, and AI. This collective effort fosters innovation and ensures that Python tools are continuously refined and optimized, benefiting everyone from beginners to experts.

For web scraping, the open-source community has created and maintained a variety of libraries, each designed to handle specific aspects of data collection. For instance, Scrapy is an open-source web scraping framework that can manage large-scale scraping projects, while BeautifulSoup focuses on simple and intuitive HTML parsing. The open-source contributions from the community ensure that these tools evolve rapidly and remain accessible to developers globally, often for free or at minimal cost.

Additionally, the community-driven nature of Python encourages collaboration, sharing of best practices, and the development of resources like tutorials, documentation, and forums, where learners and professionals can seek guidance and share their knowledge. This open-source ecosystem democratizes access to advanced tools and techniques, empowering a diverse range of people—whether individuals or organizations—to leverage Python for data extraction, analysis, and machine learning tasks.

In summary, Python's simplicity and the strength of its open-source community have made it the language of choice for web scraping, automation, data science, and machine learning. The contributions of the open-source community have accelerated the development of powerful tools, allowing professionals to tackle complex data challenges, build intelligent systems, and drive innovation across industries. By mastering Python and tapping into this ecosystem, data scientists, developers, and businesses can unlock the full potential of data to gain insights and develop impactful AI and ML applications.

Who This Book is For

Data analysts and scientists seeking to integrate web scraping into their workflows.

Developers aiming to automate repetitive tasks.

Business professionals exploring data extraction for market research and trend analysis.

Students and hobbyists interested in learning Python through practical projects.

What You Will Learn

Fundamentals of Python and OOP.

Fundamentals of web scraping and the HTTP protocol.

Python libraries and tools for web scraping and automation.

Best practices and ethical considerations.

Handling complex scenarios like dynamic websites and CAPTCHAs.

Chapter 1: Python Basics for Web Scraping

Introduction

Programming languages differ in how they execute code, categorized into **compiled**, **interpreted**, and **hybrid** approaches.

1. **Compiled languages** like C and C++ are translated directly into machine code by a compiler. This machine-specific code executes efficiently and is ideal for performance-critical applications, such as operating systems, game engines, or embedded systems. However, this efficiency comes at the cost of platform dependence; code compiled for one architecture typically won't run on another without recompilation.
2. **Interpreted languages** like Python run code through an interpreter, which translates high-level instructions into machine code at runtime. This allows for rapid development and debugging since there's no need for a separate compilation step. Python's interpreted nature makes it slower compared to compiled languages but offers unparalleled flexibility and ease of use.
3. **Hybrid languages** such as Java and C# take a middle ground. Code is first compiled into an intermediate language (e.g., Java bytecode or C# Common Intermediate Language) and then executed by a runtime environment (like the

JVM or CLR). This provides platform independence and opportunities for runtime optimization, such as Just-In-Time (JIT) compilation.

Why Python Is Good for Industry

Python has emerged as a dominant language in many industries due to its simplicity, versatility, and vast ecosystem of libraries and frameworks. Its strengths include:

- **Ease of Use**: Python's readable syntax and dynamic typing reduce the learning curve, enabling developers to quickly prototype and deploy solutions.
- **Rapid Development**: Its interpreted nature and high-level abstractions make it ideal for fast iteration cycles, crucial for startups and agile environments.
- **Extensive Ecosystem**: Python boasts robust libraries for data analysis (Pandas, NumPy), web development (Django, Flask), machine learning (TensorFlow, PyTorch), and automation.
- **Cross-Platform Compatibility**: Python code can run on various platforms with minimal changes, saving time in development and deployment.
- **Community and Support**: A vast global community ensures abundant resources, tutorials, and frameworks, making it easy to find solutions or collaborate.

From powering AI models and automating tasks to building web applications and managing large-scale data pipelines, Python's adaptability ensures its continued relevance across industries. While it might not be as fast as C++ for computation-heavy tasks, integration with optimized libraries like NumPy bridges this gap effectively.

Chapter 1.0.1: Data Types

Data types in Python define the type of value a variable can hold. Python is dynamically typed, meaning variables do not need explicit declaration of their type.

1.0.1.1 Basic Data Types

a. Integer

- Represents whole numbers.
- **Example:**
- `x = 10`
- `# Manipulation`
- `x += 5   # Increment by 5`
- `x *= 2   # Multiply by 2`
- `print(x)   # Output: 30`

b. Float

- Represents decimal numbers.
- **Example:**

- `pi = 3.14159`
- `# Manipulation`
- `pi_squared = pi ** 2  # Square the value`
- `rounded_pi = round(pi, 2)  # Round to 2 decimal places`
- `print(rounded_pi)  # Output: 3.14`

c. String

- Represents sequences of characters.
- **Example:**
- `greeting = "Hello, World!"`
- `# Manipulation`
- `uppercase_greeting = greeting.upper()  # Convert to uppercase`
- `replaced_greeting = greeting.replace("World", "Python")  # Replace substring`
- `print(replaced_greeting)  # Output: Hello, Python!`

d. Boolean

- Represents `True` or `False` values.
- **Example:**
- `is_valid = True`
- `# Manipulation`
- `is_valid = not is_valid  # Toggle the boolean value`
- `print(is_valid)  # Output: False`

1.0.1.2 Complex Data Types

a. List

- Ordered, mutable sequence of elements.
- **Example:**
- `fruits = ["apple", "banana", "cherry"]`
- `# Manipulation`
- `fruits.append("date")  # Add an element`
- `fruits.remove("banana")  # Remove an element`
- `fruits[0] = "apricot"  # Update an element`
- `print(fruits)  # Output: ['apricot', 'cherry', 'date']`

b. Tuple

- Ordered, immutable sequence of elements.
- **Example:**
- `coordinates = (10, 20)`
- `# Manipulation`
- `x, y = coordinates  # Unpack the tuple`
- `new_coordinates = coordinates + (30,)  # Create a new tuple`
- `print(new_coordinates)  # Output: (10, 20, 30)`

c. Dictionary

- Key-value pairs, mutable and unordered.
- **Example:**

```
person = {"name": "Alice", "age": 25}
# Manipulation
person["age"] = 26   # Update a value
person["city"] = "New York"   # Add a new key-value pair
del person["name"]   # Delete a key-value pair
print(person)   # Output: {'age': 26, 'city': 'New York'}
```

d. Set

- Unordered collection of unique elements.
- **Example:**
```
unique_numbers = {1, 2, 3, 4}
# Manipulation
unique_numbers.add(5)   # Add an element
unique_numbers.remove(2)   # Remove an element
unique_numbers.update({6, 7})   # Add multiple elements
print(unique_numbers)   # Output: {1, 3, 4, 5, 6, 7}
```

1.0.1.3 Type Conversion

Python allows type conversion between different data types.

- **Example:**
```
num_str = "123"
num = int(num_str)   # Converts string to integer
num_float = float(num)   # Converts integer to float
print(num_float)   # Output: 123.0
```

Chapter 1.0.2: Control Flow

Control flow structures enable decision-making, looping, and branching in programs.

1.0.2.1 Conditional Statements

a. if Statement

- **Example:**
```
if x > 0:
    print("Positive")
```

b. if-else Statement

- **Example:**
```
if x > 0:
    print("Positive")
else:
    print("Non-positive")
```

c. if-elif-else Statement

- **Example:**

- if x > 0:
-     print("Positive")
- elif x == 0:
-     print("Zero")
- else:
-     print("Negative")

1.0.2.2 Loops

a. for Loop

- **Example:**
- for i in range(5):
-     print(i)

b. while Loop

- **Example:**
- count = 0
- while count < 5:
-     print(count)
-     count += 1

1.0.2.3 Break and Continue

a. break

- **Example:**
- for i in range(10):
-     if i == 5:
-         break
-     print(i)

b. continue

- **Example:**
- for i in range(10):
-     if i % 2 == 0:
-         continue
-     print(i)

1.0.2.4 Nested Loops

- **Example:**
- for i in range(3):
-     for j in range(2):
-         print(f"i={i}, j={j}")

1.0.2.5 Exception Handling

Control flow also includes handling exceptions.

- **Example:**

- try:
-     result = 10 / 0
- except ZeroDivisionError:
-     print("Cannot divide by zero")

Chapter 1.0.3.: Mastering Object-Oriented Programming in Python

1.0.3.1. Classes and Objects

Classes and objects are the foundation of object-oriented programming (OOP). A class serves as a blueprint, while an object is an instance of that class.

- **Example:**
- class Animal:
-     def __init__(self, name):
-         self.name = name
-
-     def speak(self):
-         return "This animal makes a sound."
-
- # Creating objects
- dog = Animal("Dog")
- cat = Animal("Cat")
-
- print(dog.name)   # Output: Dog
- print(cat.speak())   # Output: This animal makes a sound.

1.0.3.2. Encapsulation

Encapsulation involves bundling data (attributes) and methods into a single unit while restricting direct access to some of an object's components.

- **Example:**
- class Animal:
-     def __init__(self, name, medical_history):
-         self.name = name
-         self.__medical_history = medical_history   # Private attribute
-
-     def get_medical_history(self):
-         return self.__medical_history
-
- # Creating an object
- pet = Animal("Dog", "No allergies")
- print(pet.get_medical_history())   # Output: No allergies

1.0.3.3. Inheritance

Inheritance allows a class (child) to acquire the properties and methods of another class (parent).

- **Example:**
- ```
  class Animal:
      def __init__(self, name):
          self.name = name

      def speak(self):
          return "This animal makes a sound."

  class Dog(Animal):
      def speak(self):
          return "Woof!"

  class Cat(Animal):
      def speak(self):
          return "Meow!"

  dog = Dog("Buddy")
  cat = Cat("Kitty")

  print(dog.speak())   # Output: Woof!
  print(cat.speak())   # Output: Meow!
  ```

1.0.3.4. Polymorphism

Polymorphism allows objects of different classes to be treated uniformly based on shared methods or attributes.

- **Example:**
- ```
  animals = [Dog("Buddy"), Cat("Kitty")]
  for animal in animals:
      print(f"{animal.name} says {animal.speak()}")
  ```

1.0.3.5. Abstraction

Abstraction focuses on exposing only relevant details while hiding implementation specifics.

- **Example:**
- ```
  from abc import ABC, abstractmethod

  class PetService(ABC):
      @abstractmethod
      def schedule_vet_appointment(self):
          pass

  class DogService(PetService):
      def schedule_vet_appointment(self):
          return "Vet appointment scheduled for the dog."

  service = DogService()
  print(service.schedule_vet_appointment())
  ```
  ```

Conclusion

Understanding Python's data types and control flow is crucial for writing efficient and effective programs. These foundational concepts form the backbone of problem-solving and logic implementation in Python.

Summary of OOP

- **Classes and Objects:** Create and manage objects using classes.
- **Encapsulation:** Protect sensitive data using private attributes.
- **Inheritance:** Reuse code by deriving new classes from existing ones.
- **Polymorphism:** Use shared methods across different objects seamlessly.
- **Abstraction:** Define abstract base classes to standardize functionality.

These principles form the core of Python's OOP capabilities, enabling you to write clean, modular, and reusable code.

Chapter 2: Introduction to Web Scraping

2.1 What is Web Scraping?

Definition: Web scraping is the automated process of extracting data from websites. Unlike manual copying and pasting, web scraping uses programs to fetch and process the required data efficiently.

How it Works (High-Level):

- Web scraping involves sending HTTP requests to a website to retrieve its HTML content.
- The HTML is parsed to extract specific data points using tools and libraries.
- The extracted data is then structured and saved for further analysis or usage.

Web Scraping vs. Web Crawling/Spidering:

- Web crawling focuses on discovering and indexing web pages, typically for search engines.
- Web scraping extracts specific data from discovered pages.

Types of Web Scraping:

- Parsing HTML/XML: Using libraries like Beautiful Soup or lxml to process static web pages.
- Using APIs: Preferred when websites offer APIs for data access, reducing ethical and technical challenges.
- Headless Browsers: Tools like Selenium or Playwright help scrape dynamic content rendered by JavaScript.

2.2 Key Use Cases

- Market Research:
  - Monitoring and comparing prices.
  - Analyzing product reviews and sentiment.
  - Identifying market trends.

- Lead Generation:
  - Collecting contact information (e.g., emails, phone numbers) ethically.
  - Creating targeted marketing lists.

- Competitive Analysis:
  - Tracking competitor pricing and offerings.
  - Monitoring marketing strategies and SEO performance.

- Other Use Cases:
  - Data journalism, academic research, real estate aggregation, and financial analysis.

2.3 Legal and Ethical Considerations

- Terms of Service and Robots.txt: Adhere to the rules in a website's robots.txt file and terms of service to respect its data usage policies.
- Rate Limiting and Avoiding Overloading Servers: Implement delays between requests to avoid overwhelming a website's servers.
- Data Privacy and GDPR/CCPA Compliance: Handle personal data responsibly to avoid legal risks associated with privacy violations.
- Copyright and Intellectual Property: Be cautious of using scraped data in ways that might infringe intellectual property rights.
- Best Practices: Follow ethical guidelines, such as avoiding restricted areas and seeking permission when needed.

2.4 Setting Up Your Environment

Python Installation and Setup Guide

1. Installing Python: Download Python from the official website: https://www.python.org/downloads/.

Follow the platform-specific instructions (Windows, macOS, Linux) for installation. Ensure that Python is added to your system's PATH during installation.

2.4.1 Writing Python Code in Your IDE

1. **Open Your IDE**: Open your installed IDE (e.g., Visual Studio Code, PyCharm, or any Python-compatible editor).
2. **Create a Python File**: In your IDE, create a new Python file (e.g., `main.py`). This is where you'll write your Python code.
3. **Write Python Code**: Now, write your Python code. Here's a simple example:

    ```python
    #python
    # Example Python code
    def greet(name):
        return f"Hello, {name}!"

    if __name__ == "__main__":
        name = input("Enter your name: ")
        print(greet(name))
    ```

4. **Explanation of the Code**:
    - `def greet(name):` defines a function called `greet` that takes one argument `name`.
    - `return f"Hello, {name}!"` returns a greeting message, using an f-string to insert the `name` variable into the string.
    - `if __name__ == "__main__":` ensures that the code inside this block will only run if this script is executed directly, not when it is imported as a module.

- `name = input("Enter your name: ")` asks the user for their name and stores it in the `name` variable.
- `print(greet(name))` prints the result of the `greet()` function.
5. **Run Your Code**: To run the Python file, open a terminal in your IDE (or use an external terminal), navigate to the directory where your `main.py` file is saved, and run:

```
python main.py
```

2.4.2 Understanding the Setup Commands

The commands you ran earlier set up your environment and dependencies. Here's a breakdown:

1. `pyenv local 3.11.3`:
    - This command specifies the local version of Python to use in your project. `pyenv` is a Python version management tool, and `3.11.3` is the version of Python you chose. By running this, all Python commands in this directory will use version 3.11.3.
2. `python -m venv .venv`:
    - This creates a virtual environment in your project directory. The `.venv` folder will contain the necessary files to isolate your Python project dependencies from the global Python environment. This is useful for managing dependencies for different projects.
3. `source .venv/bin/activate` **(for macOS/Linux)** or `.venv\Scripts\activate` **(for Windows)**:
    - This activates the virtual environment. When the virtual environment is active, any Python packages you install will be specific to this environment and not affect other projects or the global Python installation.
4. `pip install --upgrade pip`:
    - This command updates `pip` (Python's package installer) to the latest version to ensure that you can install packages correctly and without issues.
5. `pip install -r requirements_dev.txt`:
    - This installs the dependencies listed in the `requirements_dev.txt` file. This file contains a list of Python packages required for your development environment, including libraries like Flask, Django, or requests, depending on your project.

After these steps, you're ready to start writing and running Python code in your isolated environment. If you install new libraries, always make sure you activate the environment using `source .venv/bin/activate` (or `.venv\Scripts\activate` on Windows).

2. Using pip (Package Installer for Python): Once Python is installed, you can use pip to install Python libraries. For example, to install the 'requests' library, run the following

command in your terminal or command prompt:
  pip install requests

Here are some more examples of using pip to install Python libraries:

Installing specific versions of packages:

Bash
```
# Install a specific version of a package:
pip install requests==2.28.1

# Install a version greater than or equal to a specific version:
pip install numpy>=1.23.0
```

Installing multiple packages at once:

Bash
```
# Install multiple packages in one command:
pip install pandas numpy matplotlib
```

Installing packages from a requirements file:

Bash
```
# Create a requirements.txt file with the following content:
requests
beautifulsoup4
lxml

# Install all packages from the requirements file:
pip install -r requirements.txt
```

Upgrading installed packages:

Bash
```
# Upgrade all installed packages:
pip install --upgrade --upgrade-strategy eager

# Upgrade a specific package:
pip install --upgrade numpy
```

Uninstalling packages:

Bash
```
# Uninstall a package:
pip uninstall requests
```

Listing installed packages:

Bash
```
# List all installed packages:
pip list

# List outdated packages:
pip list --outdated
```

Using virtual environments:

Bash
```bash
# Create a virtual environment:
python -m venv my_env

# Activate the virtual environment (Linux/macOS):
source my_env/bin/activate

# Activate the virtual environment (Windows):
my_env\Scripts\activate

# Install packages within the virtual environment:
pip install requests

# Deactivate the virtual environment:
deactivate
```

These are just a few examples of how to use pip to manage Python packages. For more

3. Creating Virtual Environments (venv): Virtual environments are used to manage project dependencies separately from your system Python installation. To create a virtual environment, navigate to your project directory and run:

python -m venv env

Activate the virtual environment:
- Windows: bash .\env\Scripts\activate
- macOS/Linux: bash source env/bin/activate

After activation, your terminal prompt should indicate you're working inside the virtual environment.

Example 3: Creating and Using Virtual Environments with `venv`

Why use virtual environments?

- **Isolation:** Keeps project dependencies separate from system-wide Python installations, preventing conflicts.
- **Portability:** Packages a project with its specific dependencies, making it easier to share and deploy.
- **Experimentation:** Allows you to try different package versions and configurations without affecting your system Python.

Creating a Virtual Environment:

1. **Navigate to your project directory:**

    Bash

```
cd my_project
```

2. **Create a virtual environment:**

   Bash

   ```
   python -m venv env
   ```

   This command creates a new directory named `env` within your project directory. It contains a Python installation isolated from your system-wide Python.

Activating the Virtual Environment:

- **Windows:**

  Bash

  ```
  .\env\Scripts\activate
  ```

- **macOS/Linux:**

  Bash

  ```
  source env/bin/activate
  ```

  Once activated, your terminal prompt will typically change to indicate the active virtual environment.

Installing Packages:

Within the activated virtual environment, use `pip` to install packages:

Bash
```
pip install numpy pandas matplotlib
```

Deactivating the Virtual Environment:

Bash
```
deactivate
```

Additional Tips:

- **Managing Multiple Virtual Environments:** Consider using tools like `virtualenvwrapper` or `conda` to streamline the creation and management of multiple virtual environments.
- **Sharing Virtual Environments:** To share a virtual environment with others, you can include the `env` directory in your project repository.
- **Best Practices:** It's recommended to use virtual environments for all your Python projects to maintain a clean and organized development environment.

By following these steps, you can effectively create and manage virtual environments to ensure a smooth and efficient Python development experience.

4. Installing Essential Libraries: Install essential libraries for web scraping or automation using the following command:
   pip install requests beautifulsoup4 lxml selenium playwright

Example 4: Installing Essential Libraries for Web Scraping and Automation

To perform web scraping and automation tasks effectively, you'll need to install a few essential Python libraries. Here's how to install them using pip:

Bash
```
pip install requests beautifulsoup4 lxml selenium playwright
```

Breakdown of the Libraries:

1. **requests:**
   - Simplifies making HTTP requests to websites.
   - Useful for fetching web page content, submitting forms, and interacting with APIs.
2. **beautifulsoup4:**
   - Parses HTML and XML documents.
   - Extracts specific data from web pages, such as text, links, and images.
   - Works in conjunction with lxml for efficient parsing.
3. **lxml:**
   - Provides fast and efficient HTML and XML parsing.
   - Often used in combination with BeautifulSoup4 for improved performance.
4. **selenium:**
   - Controls web browsers programmatically.
   - Simulates user interactions like clicking buttons, filling forms, and navigating pages.
   - Useful for web scraping dynamic content and testing web applications.
5. **playwright:**
   - Modern automation library for web browsers.
   - Supports multiple browsers (Chrome, Firefox, WebKit) and platforms.
   - Offers features like auto-waiting, mobile emulation, and video recording.

Example Usage:

Here's a simple example of using these libraries to scrape a webpage:

Python
```
import requests
from bs4 import BeautifulSoup
```

```python
url = "https://www.example.com"
response = requests.get(url)
soup = BeautifulSoup(response.text, 'html.parser')

# Find all links on the page
links = soup.find_all('a')
for link in links:
    print(link.get('href'))
```

By combining these libraries, you can automate a wide range of tasks, from simple data extraction to complex web scraping and browser automation.

5. Code Editor/IDE (Optional): Choose an IDE or code editor to write your Python code. Recommended tools:
- VS Code: https://code.visualstudio.com/
- PyCharm: https://www.jetbrains.com/pycharm/
- Sublime Text: https://www.sublimetext.com/

These tools provide features like code completion, syntax highlighting, and debugging support for better productivity.

1. VS Code (Visual Studio Code):

- **Focus:** Open-source, lightweight, and highly customizable.
- **Features:** Code completion, syntax highlighting, debugging, built-in Git integration, extensive extension marketplace for additional functionality.
- **Screenshot:** Image of VS Code IDE [invalid URL removed]

2. PyCharm:

- **Focus:** Powerful IDE specifically designed for Python development.
- **Features:** Comprehensive code completion, refactoring tools, built-in debugger, scientific tools support, web development frameworks integration (paid version).
- **Screenshot:** Image of PyCharm IDE [invalid URL removed]

3. Sublime Text:

- **Focus:** Fast, lightweight, and highly customizable code editor.
- **Features:** Code completion through plugins, syntax highlighting, powerful search and replace functionality. Free to evaluate, but requires a license for continued use.
- **Screenshot:** Image of Sublime Text editor [invalid URL removed]

Ultimately, the best choice depends on your needs and preferences. Here's a quick guideline:

- **Beginners:** VS Code (easy to learn, good community support) or Thonny (specifically designed for beginners).

- **Intermediate:** VS Code, PyCharm (Community version)
- **Advanced/Web Development:** PyCharm (Professional version)

These are just a few examples, and there are many other excellent code editors/IDEs available. It's worth exploring some options to find the one that suits you best.

Chapter Summary

Introduced web scraping, its workflows, and distinctions from crawling. Covered key use cases like market research and lead generation. Emphasized legal and ethical considerations. Provided setup instructions for a Python development environment.

Chapter 3: Understanding HTML and the DOM

In this chapter, you'll learn the foundational concepts of HTML and the DOM (Document Object Model), which are vital for effectively navigating and extracting data from web pages during web scraping.

HTML Basics and Structure

HTML (HyperText Markup Language) forms the backbone of every web page. It defines the structure and content of web pages using a system of nested elements. A clear understanding of this structure is essential for selecting and extracting data.

1. Anatomy of an HTML Document

- The <!DOCTYPE html> Declaration: Indicates the document type and version of HTML.
- Root <html> Element: Contains all HTML content.
- The <head> Section: Includes metadata such as the title, styles, and external resources (CSS, JavaScript).
- The <body> Section: Contains the visible content displayed to users.

```html
<!DOCTYPE html>
<html>
  <head>
    <title>Web Scraping Example</title>
    <meta charset="UTF-8">
    <link rel="stylesheet" href="styles.css">
    <script src="script.js"></script>
```

```
    </head>
    <body>
      <h1>Welcome to Web Scraping</h1>
      <p>Web scraping is an essential tool for data extraction.</p>
      <ul>
         <li>Data Point 1</li>
         <li>Data Point 2</li>
      </ul>
    </body>
</html>
```

- Tags: `<h1>` for headings, `<p>` for paragraphs, `<ul>` and `<li>` for lists.
- Attributes: Tags can have attributes like id, class, style, etc., that are useful for identifying elements during scraping.

The DOM: A Tree Representation of HTML

The DOM is a tree-like representation of an HTML document. It allows programmatic access and manipulation of the structure and content.

2. DOM Structure and Relationships

- Nodes: Each element or piece of text is a node in the DOM tree.
- Hierarchy:
  - Parent Node: The element containing another element (e.g., `<body>` is the parent of `<h1>`).
  - Child Nodes: Elements nested inside a parent (e.g., `<h1>` is a child of `<body>`).
  - Siblings: Elements sharing the same parent (e.g., `<h1>` and `<p>` are siblings).

```
<html>
    ├── <head>
    │       ├── <title>
    │       └── <meta>
    └── <body>
            ├── <h1>
            ├── <p>
            └── <ul>
                    ├── <li>
                    └── <li>
```

Using Browser Developer Tools

Developer tools in modern browsers are indispensable for analyzing and understanding a webpage's structure.

1. Accessing Developer Tools

Right-click > Inspect/Inspect Element: Opens the developer tools panel.
Keyboard Shortcuts:
- Windows: Ctrl + Shift + I
- Mac: Cmd + Option + I

2. Inspecting and Navigating the DOM

Elements Tab:
- Shows the DOM structure.
- Hovering over elements highlights them on the page.
- Enables viewing and editing attributes, styles, and content in real-time.

```
<div id="info" class="data">
  <span class="value">100</span>
</div>
```

To target <span>:
  - CSS Selector: div#info .value
  - XPath: //*[@id="info"]/span

3. Network Tab for Data Analysis

Tracks HTTP requests and responses.
Useful for identifying API calls or AJAX-loaded content during scraping.

Practical Example: Extracting Data

```
from bs4 import BeautifulSoup

html = '''<div id="data-section" class="info"><span class="value">42</span></div>'''
soup = BeautifulSoup(html, 'html.parser')
value = soup.select_one('div#data-section .value').text
print(value)   # Output: 42
```

Key DOM Features

In this chapter, we will discuss some key features of the DOM and how to interact with it effectively, particularly for web scraping tasks.

Dynamic Content

JavaScript can alter the DOM after the page loads, which means that the structure of the page can change dynamically while you're scraping it.

Selectors

Selectors like CSS selectors and XPath are essential for targeting specific elements within the DOM. Tools like BeautifulSoup and Selenium make it easy to use these selectors for scraping.

1. Accessing Developer Tools:

- Right-click > Inspect/Inspect Element: Opens the developer tools panel.
- Keyboard Shortcuts:
    - Windows: Ctrl + Shift + I
    - Mac: Cmd + Option + I

2. Inspecting and Navigating the DOM:

- Elements Tab: Shows the DOM structure.
- Hovering over elements highlights them on the page.
- Enables viewing and editing attributes, styles, and content in real-time.

```html
<div id="info" class="data">
  <span class="value">100</span>
</div>
```

To target <span>:

CSS Selector: div#info .value
XPath: //*[@id="info"]/span

3. Network Tab for Data Analysis:

- Tracks HTTP requests and responses.
- Useful for identifying API calls or AJAX-loaded content during scraping.

Practical Example: Extracting Data

Imagine we want to extract the value 42 from the following HTML snippet:

```html
<div id="data-section" class="info">
  <span class="value">42</span>
</div>
```

Using developer tools:

CSS Selector: div#data-section .value
XPath: //*[@id="data-section"]/span

For scraping:

```
from bs4 import BeautifulSoup

html = '''<div id="data-section" class="info"><span class="value">42</span></div>'''
soup = BeautifulSoup(html, 'html.parser')
value = soup.select_one('div#data-section .value').text
print(value)   # Output: 42
```

HTML Sample:

```
<!DOCTYPE html>
<html>
 <head>
  <title>Sample Page</title>
 </head>
 <body>
  <div id="content">
   <h1>Welcome to Web Scraping</h1>
   <p class="description">This page demonstrates CSS selectors.</p>
   <ul class="data-list">
    <li class="item">Item 1</li>
    <li class="item">Item 2</li>
    <li class="item highlight">Item 3</li>
   </ul>
   <a href="https://example.com" class="external-link">Visit Example</a>
  </div>
  <footer>
   <p>Footer Text</p>
  </footer>
 </body>
</html>
```

Python Code Examples:

```
from bs4 import BeautifulSoup

html = '''<html>...'''   # Use the full HTML from above
```

```python
soup = BeautifulSoup(html, 'html.parser')
title = soup.select_one('title').text
print(title)  # Output: Sample Page

# Extract paragraph
description = soup.select_one('p.description').text
print(description)  # Output: This page demonstrates CSS selectors.

# Extract all list items
list_items = soup.select('ul.data-list li')
for item in list_items:
    print(item.text)
# Output:
# Item 1
# Item 2
# Item 3

# Extract highlighted item
highlighted_item = soup.select_one('li.item.highlight').text
print(highlighted_item)  # Output: Item 3

# Extract link text and URL
link = soup.select_one('a.external-link')
print(link.text)  # Output: Visit Example
print(link['href'])  # Output: https://example.com

# Extract direct child h1
header = soup.select_one('div#content > h1').text
print(header)  # Output: Welcome to Web Scraping

# Extract all descendants within #content
content_descendants = soup.select('div#content *')
for element in content_descendants:
    print(element.name)  # Outputs tag names like h1, p, ul, li, a

# Extract all class attributes of list items
list_items = soup.select('ul.data-list li')
for item in list_items:
    print(item['class'])  # Output: ['item'], ['item'], ['item', 'highlight']

# Using OR with CSS selectors
elements = soup.select('.item, .highlight')
for element in elements:
    print(element.text)
# Output:
# Item 1
# Item 2
# Item 3

# Extract element by href attribute
link = soup.select_one('a[href="https://example.com"]').text
print(link)  # Output: Visit Example

# Filter list items containing the word 'Item'
list_items = soup.select('ul.data-list li')
for item in list_items:
    if 'Item' in item.text:
        print(item.text)
```

```
# Output:
# Item 1
# Item 2
# Item 3
```

Summary

In this chapter, we learned about key DOM features and how to interact with dynamic content using selectors. We also explored how browser developer tools can help you inspect, navigate, and manipulate the DOM to extract useful data. CSS selectors and XPath are crucial for selecting elements in the DOM, and Python libraries like BeautifulSoup make it easier to scrape data.

Chapter Summary

HTML structures content and provides a roadmap for web scraping. The DOM is a manipulable representation of the webpage, enabling data extraction through tools and libraries. Developer Tools help identify and target specific elements for scraping by analyzing selectors and network activity. This knowledge sets the foundation for understanding advanced scraping techniques, handling dynamic content, and interacting with APIs in upcoming chapters.

Chapter 4: Python Basics for Web Scraping

In this chapter, we will lay the foundation for your web scraping journey by introducing essential Python concepts and libraries. Web scraping involves extracting data from web pages, and Python is a versatile language for such tasks due to its simplicity and rich ecosystem of libraries. We'll begin by installing the necessary tools, which include libraries that will help us interact with web pages and extract data from them. Next, we will cover Python fundamentals that are specifically relevant to web scraping, including variables, data types, control structures, and more. Finally, we will implement our learning by building a basic web scraper, which will fetch information from a web page.

4.1 Installing Necessary Libraries

Before we begin writing any scraping code, it's important to install the right libraries. Python's vast ecosystem of libraries makes web scraping straightforward. The following are the core libraries that will help us in this journey:

- requests

The `requests` library is one of the simplest and most popular libraries for making HTTP requests. It's used to fetch web pages, which is a fundamental part of web scraping. With `requests`, we can send HTTP requests (like GET or POST) and receive responses, including the HTML content of the pages we want to scrape.

Installation: Open your terminal or command prompt and type: `pip install requests`

- Beautiful Soup (bs4)

Beautiful Soup is a powerful library that allows us to parse HTML and XML documents. It makes navigating, searching, and modifying the parse tree easier. For web scraping, it helps us extract specific data from the HTML of a page. Beautiful Soup works with various parsers, such as Python's built-in parser and lxml, to convert the raw HTML into a readable format.

Installation: `pip install beautifulsoup4`

- lxml (Optional but Recommended)

While Beautiful Soup can parse HTML using Python's built-in parser, the `lxml` library is often recommended for its speed and efficiency when dealing with large documents. It is a fast, memory-efficient library for processing XML and HTML. Using lxml can speed up scraping tasks, especially when working with websites that have large HTML files.

Installation: `pip install lxml`

- Selenium (For Dynamic Websites)

Some websites load their content dynamically with JavaScript. This means that the data is not directly available in the HTML source code. To interact with such sites, we need tools like `Selenium`. Selenium allows us to automate a real web browser (like Chrome or Firefox), enabling us to access the content rendered by JavaScript.

Installation: `pip install selenium`

4.2 Fundamentals of Python for Data Extraction

In this section, we will review some Python fundamentals that are specifically important for web scraping. These basic concepts will form the backbone of our scraping scripts. If you already know Python, you can skim through this section; otherwise, this will serve as a valuable refresher.

- Variables and Data Types

In Python, variables are used to store values. These values can be of various types, such as: - **Strings**: Textual data (e.g., `name = "John"`)- **Integers**: Whole numbers (e.g., `age = 30`)- **Floats**: Numbers with decimal points (e.g., `price = 29.99`)- **Lists**: Ordered collections of items (e.g., `fruits = ['apple', 'banana', 'cherry']`)- **Dictionaries**: Collections of key-value pairs (e.g., `person = {'name': 'John', 'age': 30}`). These data types will be used extensively when extracting and storing data from web pages.

- Strings and String Manipulation

In web scraping, strings are a common data type we will encounter, especially when dealing with text data extracted from web pages. We can manipulate strings in Python using various methods: - **Concatenation**: Combining strings (e.g., `full_name = first_name + " " + last_name`)- **Slicing**: Extracting part of a string (e.g., `substring = text[1:5]`)- **Strip()**: Removes whitespace from the beginning and end of a string (e.g., `cleaned_text = text.strip()`). Mastering these methods will help clean and structure data.

- Lists and Dictionaries

Lists are ordered collections of items, which are useful for storing multiple values that we need to process, such as all the URLs or titles we scrape from a page. Dictionaries, on the other hand, allow us to store data in key-value pairs, making it easier to associate extracted data with its corresponding attribute (e.g., `{'title': 'Example', 'description': 'This is an example.'}`).

- Control Flow (if/else statements and loops)

Control flow structures like `if/else` statements and loops (`for` and `while`) allow us to make decisions and repeat actions in our code. These are key for processing dynamic content. For example, you may need to loop through a list of links to scrape multiple pages or check conditions (like whether an element exists) before extracting data.

- Functions

Functions allow us to encapsulate code into reusable blocks. This is especially helpful in scraping, where certain actions (like sending a request, parsing HTML, etc.) are repetitive. By writing functions, we can avoid redundancy and improve the readability and maintainability of our code.

- Working with HTML Elements

HTML elements (like `<div>`, `<a>`, `<p>`) structure the content of a web page. These elements have attributes such as `id`, `class`, and `href`, which help us identify and target specific parts of the page. For example, to extract the title of a page, we can access the `<title>` tag, and for links, we can extract the `href` attribute from the `<a>` tags.

4.3 Writing Your First Scraper

Let's implement our knowledge and build a simple web scraper. We will extract the title and a short description from a basic HTML page. If you don't have a simple HTML file, you can use a static example site or any basic page that doesn't change dynamically.

Code Example:

```
bs4 import BeautifulSoup

url = "YOUR_EXAMPLE_WEBSITE_URL"  # Replace with your example URL

try:
    response = requests.get(url)
    response.raise_for_status()  # Raise an exception for bad status codes (4xx or 5xx)

    soup = BeautifulSoup(response.content, "lxml")  # Use lxml for parsing

    title = soup.title.text  # Extract the title
    description = soup.find("meta", attrs={"name": "description"})["content"] if soup.find("meta", attrs={"name": "description"}) else "No description found"  # Extract the description (handling cases where it might not exist)

    print(f"Title: {title}")
    print(f"Description: {description}")

except requests.exceptions.RequestException as e:
    print(f"Error fetching URL: {e}")
except AttributeError as e:
    print(f"Error parsing HTML: {e}. Check if the elements exist on the page.")
except TypeError as e:
    print(f"Error handling description: {e}. Description tag might not be present")
```

Explanation:

Here's a step-by-step explanation of the code:

- 1. **Importing libraries**: We start by importing `requests` to handle HTTP requests and `BeautifulSoup` from `bs4` to parse the HTML.
- 2. **Sending a request**: `requests.get(url)` sends an HTTP GET request to the specified URL, retrieving the page content.
- 3. **Error handling**: We use `response.raise_for_status()` to check for any errors in the HTTP response (e.g., 404 or 500). If there's an error, it will raise an exception.
- 4. **Parsing HTML**: We create a `BeautifulSoup` object (`soup`) to parse the HTML content. The `lxml` parser is used here for speed.
- 5. **Extracting data**: The title is extracted using `soup.title.text`. To get the description, we use `soup.find()`, which searches for a `<meta>` tag with the name attribute set to 'description'. If the meta tag doesn't exist, a default value 'No description found' is returned.
- 6. **Printing results**: Finally, we print the extracted title and description to the console.

- 7. **Handling errors**: We use `try...except` blocks to handle errors that might occur during the scraping process, such as network issues or missing elements in the HTML.

Chapter Summary

In this chapter, we introduced the key Python tools and libraries for web scraping. We installed `requests`, `Beautiful Soup`, `lxml`, and `Selenium`, and we explored important Python concepts like variables, strings, lists, and functions. We also wrote our first simple scraper that extracts data from a web page. In the next chapter, we will explore more advanced techniques for scraping dynamic content and handling more complex scenarios.

Chapter 5: Using BeautifulSoup for Static Pages

5.1 Extracting Data from Static HTML

Understanding Static Pages:
Static pages are web pages where the content is fixed and does not change unless the HTML code itself is modified. This makes them predictable and easier to scrape because the structure remains the same every time you access the page.
Examples include simple blogs, informational websites, and some e-commerce product pages.

Parsing HTML with BeautifulSoup:

BeautifulSoup is a Python library used for parsing HTML and XML documents. It creates a parse tree for parsed pages that can be used to extract data easily.
To use BeautifulSoup, you first need to load the HTML content, which can be done using Python's requests library to fetch the page content.
Once loaded, you can navigate the DOM (Document Object Model) using BeautifulSoup's methods to find and extract the data you need.

Example:

Suppose you want to extract product details like name, price, and description from an e-commerce site. You would:
1. Fetch the HTML content of the product page.
2. Use BeautifulSoup to parse the HTML.
3. Locate the elements containing the product details using tags, classes, or IDs.

5.2 Navigating and Searching the DOM

Navigating the DOM:

BeautifulSoup provides several methods to navigate the DOM:
.find(): Finds the first occurrence of a tag.
.find_all(): Finds all occurrences of a tag.
CSS selectors: Use select() to find elements using CSS selectors.

Searching for Elements:

You can search for elements by:
Tag: e.g., <div>, <a>, <span>.
Class: Use the class_ parameter to find elements with a specific class.
ID: Use the id parameter to find elements with a specific ID.
Attributes: Use the attrs parameter to search for elements with specific attributes.

Example:

To extract all links from a webpage, you would:
1. Use .find_all('a') to get all anchor tags.
2. Extract the href attribute from each tag to get the URLs.

5.3 Handling Common Challenges

Pagination:

Many websites spread their content across multiple pages. To scrape such sites, you need to handle pagination.
This involves identifying the pattern in the URLs of different pages or finding the 'next' button/link and iterating over pages until you reach the end.

Handling Missing Data:

Sometimes, the data you expect might be missing or incomplete. You can handle this by:
Using try-except blocks to catch exceptions.
Checking if an element exists before trying to access its content.

Example:

When scraping a blog with multiple pages of posts, you would:
1. Start from the first page and extract the posts.
2. Look for a 'next' button or link to navigate to the next page.
3. Repeat the process until there are no more pages.

Complete Example: Scraping Data with BeautifulSoup

Python Code Example:

```python
import requests
from bs4 import BeautifulSoup

# Step 1: Fetch the HTML content of the product page
url = 'https://www.example.com/product-page'  # Replace with the actual URL of the product page
response = requests.get(url)
response.raise_for_status()  # Check if the request was successful

# Step 2: Parse the HTML content using BeautifulSoup
soup = BeautifulSoup(response.text, 'html.parser')

# Step 3: Extract product details
# Find the product name
product_name = soup.find('h1', {'class': 'product-name'}).text.strip()
# Find the product price
product_price = soup.find('span', {'class': 'product-price'}).text.strip()
# Find the product description
product_description = soup.find('div', {'class': 'product-description'}).text.strip()

# Step 4: Print out the extracted data
print(f"Product Name: {product_name}")
print(f"Product Price: {product_price}")
print(f"Product Description: {product_description}")
```

Explanation of Each Step:

1. Import Necessary Libraries:
   o requests: A library to send HTTP requests to fetch HTML content.
   o BeautifulSoup: Part of the bs4 library, which helps in parsing HTML/XML content.
2. Step 1: Fetch the HTML content of the product page:
   o url = 'https://www.example.com/product-page': Specify the URL of the product page you want to scrape.
   o response = requests.get(url): Sends a GET request to the specified URL to retrieve the HTML content.
   o response.raise_for_status(): Checks if the request was successful (raises an exception if there was an error).
3. Step 2: Parse the HTML content using BeautifulSoup:
   o soup = BeautifulSoup(response.text, 'html.parser'): Parses the HTML content retrieved in Step 1 using BeautifulSoup.

4. Step 3: Extract product details:
   - product_name = soup.find('h1', {'class': 'product-name'}).text.strip(): Finds the <h1> tag with the class product-name, extracts the text, and removes whitespace.
   - product_price = soup.find('span', {'class': 'product-price'}).text.strip(): Finds the <span> tag with the class product-price, extracts the text, and removes whitespace.
   - product_description = soup.find('div', {'class': 'product-description'}).text.strip(): Finds the <div> tag with the class product-description, extracts the text, and removes whitespace.
5. Step 4: Print out the extracted data:
   - print(f"Product Name: {product_name}"): Prints the product name.
   - print(f"Product Price: {product_price}"): Prints the product price.
   - print(f"Product Description: {product_description}"): Prints the product description.

Chapter BS4 Poupular methods

```python
#python
import requests
from bs4 import BeautifulSoup

# Step 1: Fetch the HTML content of the product page
url = 'https://www.example.com/product-page'  # Replace with the actual URL of the product page
response = requests.get(url)
response.raise_for_status()  # Check if the request was successful

# Step 2: Parse the HTML content using BeautifulSoup
soup = BeautifulSoup(response.text, 'html.parser')

# Step 3: Extract product details using different BeautifulSoup methods and properties

# 1. Find the product name using .find()
product_name = soup.find('h1', {'class': 'product-name'}).text.strip()

# 2. Find the product price using .find()
product_price = soup.find('span', {'class': 'product-price'}).text.strip()

# 3. Find the product description using .find()
product_description = soup.find('div', {'class': 'product-description'}).text.strip()

# 4. Find all links on the page using .find_all()
links = soup.find_all('a')

# 5. Extract the href attribute of all links
hrefs = [link.get('href') for link in links]

# 6. Use .select() to find an element by CSS selector
image_url = soup.select('img.product-image')[0].get('src')

# 7. Get the title of the page using .title
page_title = soup.title.string.strip()

# 8. Get the page's HTML structure using .prettify()
pretty_html = soup.prettify()
```

```python
# 9. Find all images with a specific class
images = soup.find_all('img', {'class': 'product-image'})

# 10. Find the first div with a specific id
main_content = soup.find('div', {'id': 'main-content'})

# 11. Find the first occurrence of a tag using .find()
first_paragraph = soup.find('p')

# 12. Get the text content of an element using .text
product_text = soup.find('div', {'class': 'product-description'}).text

# 13. Use .attrs to access an element's attributes (e.g., 'src' or 'href')
image_src = soup.find('img', {'class': 'product-image'}).attrs['src']

# 14. Use .parent to navigate to the parent element of a tag
parent_element = soup.find('span', {'class': 'product-price'}).parent

# 15. Use .children to access all direct children of a tag
children_elements = soup.find('div', {'class': 'product-description'}).children

# 16. Use .next_sibling to get the next sibling of a tag
next_sibling = soup.find('h1', {'class': 'product-name'}).next_sibling

# 17. Use .previous_sibling to get the previous sibling of a tag
previous_sibling = soup.find('h1', {'class': 'product-name'}).previous_sibling

# 18. Use .find_all('tag', limit=n) to limit the number of results
limited_images = soup.find_all('img', limit=5)

# 19. Get the number of occurrences of a tag with .find_all()
num_links = len(soup.find_all('a'))

# 20. Get the first match of a tag using .find_all() with conditions
first_button = soup.find_all('button', {'class': 'buy-now'})[0]

# Step 4: Print out the extracted data
print(f"Product Name: {product_name}")
print(f"Product Price: {product_price}")
print(f"Product Description: {product_description}")
print(f"All Links: {hrefs}")
print(f"Image URL: {image_url}")
print(f"Page Title: {page_title}")
print(f"Pretty HTML: {pretty_html[:500]}...")  # Show first 500 chars for preview
print(f"Images: {[img['src'] for img in images]}")
print(f"Main Content: {main_content}")
print(f"First Paragraph: {first_paragraph.text}")
print(f"Product Text: {product_text}")
print(f"Image Src: {image_src}")
print(f"Parent Element: {parent_element}")
print(f"Children Elements: {list(children_elements)}")
print(f"Next Sibling: {next_sibling}")
print(f"Previous Sibling: {previous_sibling}")
print(f"Limited Images: {[img['src'] for img in limited_images]}")
print(f"Number of Links: {num_links}")
```

```
print(f"First Button: {first_button}")
```

Explanation of Each Method and Property:

1. **.find()**: Finds the first occurrence of a tag matching the specified criteria.
2. **.find_all()**: Finds all occurrences of a tag matching the specified criteria.
3. **.select()**: Finds elements using CSS selectors (more flexible for complex queries).
4. **.title**: Retrieves the title tag content of the webpage.
5. **.prettify()**: Returns a nicely indented version of the HTML (helpful for debugging).
6. **.attrs**: Access the attributes of a tag (e.g., `href`, `src`).
7. **.parent**: Returns the parent element of the current tag.
8. **.children**: Access all direct children of a tag.
9. **.next_sibling**: Access the next sibling tag of the current element.
10. **.previous_sibling**: Access the previous sibling tag of the current element.
11. **.text**: Extracts the text content of an element.
12. **.get()**: Retrieves the value of a tag's attribute (e.g., `get('href')` for a link).
13. **.select_one()**: Retrieves the first element matching a CSS selector.
14. **.string**: Extracts the inner text of a tag.
15. **.find_all('tag', limit=n)**: Limits the number of results returned by `.find_all()`.
16. **.name**: Retrieves the name of a tag (e.g., `<a>` returns `'a'`).
17. **.descendants**: Iterates over all descendant tags of the element.
18. **.parent**: Returns the parent tag of the current element.
19. **.next()**: Gets the next tag or element in the document.
20. **.previous()**: Gets the previous tag or element in the document.

Use Cases for These Methods:

- **.find() and .find_all()**: Used when you want to extract specific elements (like product names, links, or images) by searching for their tags and attributes.
- **.select()**: Allows for more sophisticated querying, especially when dealing with complex HTML structures.
- **.attrs and .get()**: Used for accessing the attributes of HTML elements like `href` for links or `src` for images.
- **.parent, .children, .next_sibling**: Useful for navigating around the DOM, for example, when you need to find related data or elements in the same hierarchy.
- **.prettify()**: Great for debugging or pretty-printing the HTML content.
- **.text**: Extracts only the visible text from an HTML element, useful for content scraping (e.g., product descriptions or blog post text).
- **.limit in .find_all()**: Limits the number of results you get when you only need a small sample.

This set of methods and properties should give you a comprehensive approach to scraping with BeautifulSoup, allowing you to extract, navigate, and manipulate HTML content efficiently.

Chapter Summary

This chapter provides a foundational understanding of using BeautifulSoup to extract data from static HTML pages. It covers how to navigate the DOM, search for elements, and handle challenges like pagination and missing data, making it a valuable tool for web scraping tasks.

Chapter 6: Scraping Dynamic Websites with Selenium

6.1 Introduction to Selenium for Browser Automation

What is Selenium?:
Selenium is a powerful tool for automating web browsers. It is primarily used for automating testing, but it's also very useful for web scraping dynamic websites where content is generated or modified by JavaScript.
Selenium allows you to simulate a real user's interactions with the browser, such as clicking buttons, filling out forms, and waiting for elements to load.

Setting Up Selenium:

To use Selenium, you need to install it and set up a WebDriver.

1. Install Selenium using pip:

   pip install selenium

2. Download the appropriate WebDriver (e.g., ChromeDriver) based on your browser version.
3. Ensure that the WebDriver executable is in your PATH or provide its location in your script.

Example: Automating a login process on a website:

```
from selenium import webdriver
from selenium.webdriver.common.by import By
from selenium.webdriver.common.keys import Keys

# Set up the WebDriver (ensure you have downloaded the correct driver)
driver = webdriver.Chrome(executable_path='path_to_chromedriver')  # Replace with your chromedriver path

# Open the website
driver.get('https://www.example.com/login')

# Locate the username and password fields and input credentials
username = driver.find_element(By.ID, 'username')
password = driver.find_element(By.ID, 'password')

username.send_keys('your_username')
password.send_keys('your_password')

# Simulate pressing the Enter key to submit the form
password.send_keys(Keys.RETURN)

# Close the browser
driver.quit()
```

6.2 Handling JavaScript-Rendered Content

Understanding Dynamic Content:
Many modern websites use JavaScript to load content dynamically after the initial page load. This can include data from AJAX calls or interactive elements that are not present in the HTML at first.
When scraping such websites, you need to wait for the dynamic content to load before extracting the data.

Using Selenium to Wait for Content:

Selenium provides methods like `WebDriverWait` and `expected_conditions` to handle dynamic content. These allow you to wait for elements to be present, visible, or clickable before interacting with them.

Example:

```python
from selenium import webdriver
from selenium.webdriver.common.by import By
from selenium.webdriver.support.ui import WebDriverWait
from selenium.webdriver.support import expected_conditions as EC

# Set up the WebDriver
driver = webdriver.Chrome(executable_path='path_to_chromedriver')

# Open the website
driver.get('https://www.example.com')

# Wait until a specific element is visible (e.g., a product listing)
wait = WebDriverWait(driver, 10)
element = wait.until(EC.visibility_of_element_located((By.ID, 'product-list')))

# Extract data once the element is visible
print(element.text)

# Close the browser
driver.quit()
```

6.3 Interacting with Forms, Buttons, and Dropdowns

Form Interactions:
Selenium allows you to interact with forms on websites by filling out fields and submitting them. You can locate form elements like text fields, radio buttons, checkboxes, and submit buttons, then automate their interaction.

Clicking Buttons and Links:
You can simulate clicking buttons and links by finding them using methods like `.find_element` and `.click()`.

Handling Dropdowns:
Selenium can also interact with dropdown menus, allowing you to select options programmatically.

Example: Filling out and submitting a search form:

```python
from selenium import webdriver
from selenium.webdriver.common.by import By
from selenium.webdriver.support.ui import Select

# Set up the WebDriver
driver = webdriver.Chrome(executable_path='path_to_chromedriver')
```

```python
# Open the website
driver.get('https://www.example.com')

# Find the search form and fill in the search query
search_box = driver.find_element(By.ID, 'search-box')
search_box.send_keys('Web scraping tutorial')

# Select an option from a dropdown menu
dropdown = Select(driver.find_element(By.ID, 'category-dropdown'))
dropdown.select_by_visible_text('Technology')

# Submit the form
search_box.submit()

# Close the browser
driver.quit()
```

Chapter Summary

This chapter introduces Selenium for scraping dynamic websites, focusing on handling JavaScript-rendered content and interacting with web elements like forms, buttons, and dropdowns. Selenium provides powerful tools for automating browser interactions, making it an essential tool for scraping dynamic content.

Chapter 7: Advanced Web Scraping Techniques

7.1 Handling CAPTCHAs

CAPTCHAs (Completely Automated Public Turing test to tell Computers and Humans Apart) are used to prevent bots from accessing websites. They can be in the form of image recognition, text, or more advanced challenges such as reCAPTCHA.

Methods to Bypass CAPTCHAs:

- Manual Input: In some cases, you may need to manually solve CAPTCHAs.
- Automated CAPTCHA Solvers: Tools like 2Captcha, Anti-Captcha, and DeathByCaptcha can be used to automate CAPTCHA solving. They usually require integration via API and come with a cost.
- Headless Browsers: Tools like Selenium can be used to interact with CAPTCHAs. While they can't solve CAPTCHAs directly, they can mimic user behavior to bypass simple CAPTCHAs.
- Service Providers: External CAPTCHA solving services (like 2Captcha) can be integrated into your scraper to bypass CAPTCHA checks automatically.

```
import requests
from twocaptcha import TwoCaptcha

solver = TwoCaptcha("YOUR_2CAPTCHA_API_KEY")

def solve_captcha(captcha_image_url):
    result = solver.normal(captcha_image_url)
    return result["code"]

# Fetch CAPTCHA image URL
captcha_image_url = "https://www.example.com/captcha.png"
```

```python
# Solve the CAPTCHA
captcha_code = solve_captcha(captcha_image_url)

# Now use the solved CAPTCHA code to submit the form
response = requests.post("https://www.example.com/form", data={"captcha": captcha_code})
print(response.text)
```

7.2 Rotating User Agents and Proxies

User Agents: Websites often check the User-Agent header to detect if requests are coming from automated bots. To mimic real browsers, it's essential to rotate user agents to avoid being detected.

Using Proxies: To avoid getting blocked based on your IP address, rotating proxies can help distribute the requests across multiple IPs, reducing the risk of bans.

Proxy Rotation Strategy:

- Static Proxies: Using a fixed set of proxies for a scraper. Not ideal as it increases the likelihood of IP bans.
- Dynamic Proxies: Changing IPs frequently to evade detection. This can be achieved by using proxy services like ScraperAPI, ProxyMesh, or free proxy lists.

```python
import requests
import random

# List of user agents
user_agents = [
    "Mozilla/5.0 (Windows NT 10.0; Win64; x64) AppleWebKit/537.36 (KHTML, like Gecko) Chrome/91.0.4472.124 Safari/537.36",
    "Mozilla/5.0 (Windows NT 6.1; WOW64; rv:35.0) Gecko/20100101 Firefox/35.0",
    "Mozilla/5.0 (Windows NT 6.1; WOW64; rv:40.0) Gecko/20100101 Firefox/40.0"
]

# List of proxy addresses
proxies = [
    "http://proxy1.example.com:8080",
    "http://proxy2.example.com:8080",
    "http://proxy3.example.com:8080"
]

# Function to send requests with rotation of user agents and proxies
def fetch_page(url):
    headers = {"User-Agent": random.choice(user_agents)}
```

```
    proxy = {"http": random.choice(proxies), "https":
random.choice(proxies)}
    response = requests.get(url, headers=headers, proxies=proxy)
    return response

# Example usage
url = "https://www.example.com"
page = fetch_page(url)
print(page.status_code)
```

7.3 Managing Sessions and Cookies

Session Management: Maintaining sessions is essential when scraping websites that require login, such as social media platforms, email services, or other sites that require authentication. Sessions ensure that login information is maintained across multiple requests.

Handling Cookies: Cookies are small pieces of data that websites store on a client's computer to remember information. You can use cookies to maintain a session and stay logged in as you scrape.

```
import requests

# Start a session
session = requests.Session()

# Login data
login_data = {
    "username": "my_username",
    "password": "my_password"
}

# Login URL
login_url = "https://www.example.com/login"

# Post login data to the site
login_response = session.post(login_url, data=login_data)

# After logging in, the session cookie is maintained automatically

# Now you can use the session to scrape authenticated pages
scrape_url = "https://www.example.com/dashboard"
dashboard_response = session.get(scrape_url)

# Print the scraped content
print(dashboard_response.text)
```

Chapter Summary

This chapter delves into advanced web scraping techniques, providing solutions to common challenges faced while scraping modern websites:

CAPTCHA Handling: It covers methods for bypassing CAPTCHAs, including automated solvers and headless browser techniques.
Rotating User Agents and Proxies: We learned how to implement user agent rotation and use proxies to avoid detection and IP bans.
Managing Sessions and Cookies: This section explained how to maintain login sessions using cookies, making it easier to scrape websites that require authentication.

By using these techniques, web scrapers can avoid common blocking methods and scrape dynamic websites efficiently while maintaining ethical standards.

Chapter 8: Data Cleaning and Storage

8.1 Cleaning Scraped Data

Data cleaning is one of the most critical steps when working with scraped data, as raw data is often unstructured, messy, and inconsistent. Cleaning data ensures that it's suitable for analysis, storage, and visualization. In this section, we will explore the process of cleaning scraped data using Python libraries, specifically focusing on pandas and regex.

Using Python Libraries for Data Cleaning
pandas is one of the most powerful and widely used libraries for data manipulation and cleaning in Python. It provides easy-to-use data structures and tools for cleaning, transforming, and analyzing data. Here's how pandas can help in cleaning scraped data:

```
import pandas as pd

df = pd.read_csv('scraped_data.csv')
```

Handling Missing Values: It's common for scraped data to have missing or null values. In pandas, you can identify missing values and handle them in several ways.

```
df.isnull().sum()   # Returns a count of missing values in each column
df['column_name'].fillna(df['column_name'].mean(), inplace=True)
df.dropna(subset=['column_name'], inplace=True)
```

```
df.rename(columns={'old_name': 'new_name'}, inplace=True)
df['price'] = df['price'].astype(float)
```

Scraped data is often inconsistent. For example, product names may have leading or trailing spaces, dates may be in different formats, or currency symbols may vary across records. Here are some techniques for dealing with such inconsistencies:

```
df['product_name'] = df['product_name'].str.strip()
```

```python
df['date'] = pd.to_datetime(df['date'], format='%Y-%m-%d')
df['product_name'] = df['product_name'].str.replace(r'\W', ' ', regex=True)
df['price'] = df['price'].str.extract(r'(\d+\.\d{2})')
```

It's common for scraped data to have duplicate rows, especially if multiple pages were scraped. You can identify and drop duplicates using pandas.

```python
df.drop_duplicates(inplace=True)
```

Example: Cleaning a Dataset of Scraped Product Reviews
Suppose you have a dataset of product reviews scraped from an e-commerce site. The dataset contains columns such as 'review_date', 'review_text', 'product_name', and 'rating'. Here's how you might clean it:

```python
df.drop_duplicates(subset=['product_name', 'review_date'], inplace=True)
df['review_text'].fillna('No review provided', inplace=True)
df['product_name'] = df['product_name'].str.strip().str.title()
df['rating'] = pd.to_numeric(df['rating'], errors='coerce')
```

8.2 Storing Data in CSV, Excel, and Databases

After cleaning the scraped data, the next step is to store it in a structured format for future use. You can store data in various formats, such as CSV, Excel, or in a database like SQLite.

CSV Files: CSV (Comma-Separated Values) is a popular format for storing tabular data. pandas provides easy-to-use functions to export data to CSV.

```python
df.to_csv('cleaned_data.csv', index=False)
```

Excel Files: Sometimes you may need to store data in Excel format for further analysis or sharing with others. pandas makes this process straightforward using the to_excel() method.

```python
df.to_excel('cleaned_data.xlsx', index=False)
```

For more complex data, or if you plan to scale your data storage, using a database is often the better choice. SQLite is a lightweight, file-based database that can be easily integrated with pandas.

```python
import sqlite3

conn = sqlite3.connect('scraped_data.db')
c = conn.cursor()

c.execute('''CREATE TABLE IF NOT EXISTS product_reviews (id INTEGER PRIMARY KEY, product_name TEXT, review_date TEXT, rating REAL, review_text TEXT)''')
```

```python
df.to_sql('product_reviews', conn, if_exists='replace', index=False)
query = 'SELECT * FROM product_reviews WHERE rating > 4'
df_high_rated = pd.read_sql(query, conn)
```

8.3 Visualizing Data

Once the data is cleaned and stored, the next step is to extract meaningful insights by visualizing the data. Visualization allows you to identify trends, patterns, and outliers in the data, making it easier to draw conclusions.

Two of the most popular Python libraries for data visualization are matplotlib and seaborn. Both libraries integrate well with pandas and allow you to create a variety of plots.

```python
import matplotlib.pyplot as plt

plt.plot(df['date'], df['price'])
plt.title('Price Over Time')
plt.xlabel('Date')
plt.ylabel('Price')
plt.show()

import seaborn as sns

sns.barplot(x='product_name', y='rating', data=df)
plt.xticks(rotation=90)
plt.show()
```

Line Chart: Ideal for visualizing trends over time (e.g., product prices over several days).

```python
df['date'] = pd.to_datetime(df['date'])
df.groupby('date')['price'].mean().plot(kind='line')
plt.title('Average Price Over Time')
plt.show()

df['rating'].plot(kind='hist', bins=5, alpha=0.7)
plt.title('Rating Distribution')
plt.xlabel('Rating')
plt.show()

correlation_matrix = df.corr()
sns.heatmap(correlation_matrix, annot=True, cmap='coolwarm')
plt.title('Correlation Heatmap')
plt.show()
```

Example: Plotting Price Trends from Scraped E-Commerce Data

```python
df['date'] = pd.to_datetime(df['date'])
df_sorted = df.sort_values(by='date')

plt.figure(figsize=(10, 5))
plt.plot(df_sorted['date'], df_sorted['price'], marker='o', color='b', label='Price')
plt.title('Price Trend Over Time')
plt.xlabel('Date')
plt.ylabel('Price')
plt.legend()
```

```
plt.xticks(rotation=45)
plt.show()
```

Chapter Summary

This chapter delves into the essential steps of cleaning and storing scraped data, followed by visualizing it to gain insights. Using Python libraries like pandas and regex, we demonstrated how to clean data by handling missing values, dealing with inconsistencies, and correcting errors. We then explored the different ways of storing data, including exporting to CSV, Excel, and using databases such as SQLite. Finally, we highlighted how to use matplotlib and seaborn to visualize trends and patterns in the data, allowing you to derive meaningful insights from the scraped content.

Chapter 9: Automating Tasks

9.1 Automating Repetitive Tasks

Automating repetitive tasks, such as web scraping, is essential for many use cases. Python, with its libraries, makes it easy to automate data extraction tasks. In this section, we will write a script that scrapes news articles from a website and stores them for future use.

Step 1: Setting Up Python

Before starting, ensure you have Python installed, and then install the necessary libraries:

```
bash
```

```
pip install requests beautifulsoup4
```

Step 2: Writing the Web Scraping Script

Here is an example Python script that scrapes articles from a news website:

```python
import requests
from bs4 import BeautifulSoup

# URL of the website to scrape
url = "https://example-news-website.com"

# Send HTTP request to the website
response = requests.get(url)

# Parse the content using BeautifulSoup
soup = BeautifulSoup(response.text, 'html.parser')

# Extract all article titles
articles = soup.find_all('h2', class_='article-title')

# Loop through each article and print its title and link
for article in articles:
    title = article.text.strip()
    link = article.find('a')['href']
    print(f"Title: {title}")
    print(f"Link: {link}")
    print("-" * 50)
```

Step 3: Saving the Data to a File

Instead of just printing the results, we can save the data into a CSV file:

```python
import csv

# Open or create a CSV file to store the data
with open('articles.csv', 'w', newline='') as file:
    writer = csv.writer(file)
    writer.writerow(['Title', 'Link'])  # Write header

    # Write the data for each article
    for article in articles:
        title = article.text.strip()
        link = article.find('a')['href']
        writer.writerow([title, link])

print("Data saved to articles.csv")
```

9.2 Scheduling Scrapers

Using Cron Jobs: Setting Up Cron Jobs on Unix-Based Systems

Cron jobs are used to automate tasks on Unix-based systems (Linux and macOS). You can set up a cron job to run a Python script at regular intervals, like every hour.

Step 1: Edit the Crontab

First, open the crontab configuration by running the following command in your terminal:

```bash
crontab -e
```

This will open the crontab file for editing. To schedule a script to run every hour, you can add the following line:

```bash
0 * * * * /usr/bin/python3 /path/to/your/script.py
```

Explanation:

- `0 * * * *`: This means the script will run every hour at the 0th minute.
- `/usr/bin/python3`: Path to the Python 3 interpreter.
- `/path/to/your/script.py`: Full path to your Python script.

Task Schedulers for Windows: Using Task Scheduler to Automate Script Execution

On Windows, you can automate tasks using Task Scheduler. Here's how to set it up:

Step 1: Open Task Scheduler

Press `Win + R`, type `taskschd.msc`, and press Enter to open Task Scheduler.
In the right-hand panel, click "Create Basic Task."

Step 2: Configure the Task

1. Name your task (e.g., "Scrape News Website").
2. Choose the frequency, such as "Daily" or "Hourly."
3. Set the start time and recurrence options.
4. In the "Action" section, select "Start a Program."
5. Browse for the Python executable (`python.exe`), and in the "Add arguments" box, enter the path to your script (`/path/to/your/script.py`).

After you finish setting up the task, it will run automatically at the defined intervals.

9.3 Sending Alerts and Notifications

Email Notifications: Sending Email Alerts Based on Scraped Data

Sometimes you may want to send email alerts based on the data scraped. For instance, you could send an email when a new article about a particular topic is published.

Step 1: Install the Required Libraries

To send emails, you'll need `smtplib` and `email`. The following code uses Gmail's SMTP server:

```bash
pip install secure-smtplib
```

Step 2: Sending an Email Notification

Here's the Python code to send an email notification:

```python
import smtplib
from email.mime.text import MIMEText
from email.mime.multipart import MIMEMultipart

def send_email(subject, body, to_email):
    # Email credentials
    from_email = "your_email@gmail.com"
    from_password = "your_password"

    # Create the email message
    msg = MIMEMultipart()
    msg['From'] = from_email
    msg['To'] = to_email
    msg['Subject'] = subject

    # Attach the email body
    msg.attach(MIMEText(body, 'plain'))

    # Set up the SMTP server
    server = smtplib.SMTP('smtp.gmail.com', 587)
    server.starttls()
    server.login(from_email, from_password)

    # Send the email
    server.sendmail(from_email, to_email, msg.as_string())
    server.quit()

# Example usage
send_email("New Article Alert", "Check out the latest news on Python development.", "recipient@example.com")
```

Chapter Summary

This chapter covers automating tasks using Python, specifically for web scraping. We began by writing a Python script to scrape data from a website. Next, we discussed scheduling these tasks using cron jobs for Unix-based systems and Task Scheduler for Windows. Finally, we explored sending alerts based on specific conditions by integrating with email services and SMS APIs like Twilio.

By automating tasks, we can efficiently gather data, save it, and receive alerts whenever certain conditions are met. This reduces manual effort and helps build more responsive systems for continuous data collection and monitoring.

To create a well-structured and explanatory document for this chapter in a .docx format, I will break down each section into multiple pages and explain key concepts in detail. I'll also format the text to make it clear and easy to follow. Below is the outline for each part, and you can copy this into a word processor like Microsoft Word to apply the formatting.

Chapter 10: Case Studies and Projects

This chapter introduces you to practical web scraping and automation projects designed to solidify your understanding of web scraping concepts. By working on projects using libraries like **BeautifulSoup**, **Selenium**, and **pandas**, you will gain hands-on experience and build real-world skills.

10.1 Project 1: Building a Market Trend Scraper

Objective:

The goal of this project is to scrape data that allows for the analysis of market trends, such as tracking stock or product prices over time. This will give you the ability to monitor how prices change and identify trends in various industries.

Tools and Techniques:

- **BeautifulSoup** for parsing HTML and scraping static content.

- **pandas** for data manipulation and analysis.

Python Code Example:

```python
import requests
from bs4 import BeautifulSoup
import pandas as pd

# Step 1: Send a request to the website
url = 'https://example.com/market-trends'
response = requests.get(url)

# Step 2: Parse the HTML content
soup = BeautifulSoup(response.text, 'html.parser')

# Step 3: Extract data (example: product prices)
products = []
prices = []
for product_div in soup.find_all('div', class_='product'):
    product_name = product_div.find('span', class_='product-name').text
    price = product_div.find('span', class_='price').text
    products.append(product_name)
    prices.append(price)

# Step 4: Convert data to a pandas DataFrame
data = pd.DataFrame({
    'Product': products,
    'Price': prices
})

# Step 5: Analyze the data (example: calculating average price)
data['Price'] = data['Price'].replace({'\$': '', ',': ''}, regex=True).astype(float)
average_price = data['Price'].mean()

# Output the analysis
print(f"Average Price: ${average_price:.2f}")
```

Explanation of Code:

1. **Sending Requests:** The `requests.get(url)` method fetches the content of the target webpage.
2. **Parsing the Content:** `BeautifulSoup` is used to parse the HTML content of the page. This allows you to extract specific data, such as product names and prices.
3. **Data Extraction:** Using the `find_all()` method, we extract relevant information from each product listing.
4. **Data Conversion:** We use **pandas** to convert the extracted data into a structured format, making it easy to analyze.
5. **Data Analysis:** The code includes a simple analysis to calculate the average product price.

10.2 Project 2: Automating Price Comparison for E-commerce

Objective:

This project focuses on scraping prices from multiple e-commerce websites for a specific product and then comparing them to identify the best price.

Tools and Techniques:

- **Selenium** for handling dynamic content (i.e., JavaScript-loaded pages).
- **pandas** for data comparison.

Python Code Example:

```python
from selenium import webdriver
from selenium.webdriver.common.by import By
import pandas as pd

# Step 1: Set up Selenium WebDriver
driver = webdriver.Chrome(executable_path='/path/to/chromedriver')

# Step 2: Visit multiple e-commerce websites
urls = ['https://example.com/product-page1',
'https://example.com/product-page2']
product_prices = []

for url in urls:
    driver.get(url)

    # Wait for the page to load (or use WebDriverWait for more complex loading)
    driver.implicitly_wait(10)

    # Step 3: Extract the price for the product
    try:
        price = driver.find_element(By.CLASS_NAME, 'price').text
        product_prices.append(price)
    except Exception as e:
        product_prices.append(None)

# Step 4: Store the data in a pandas DataFrame
data = pd.DataFrame({
    'Product Page': urls,
    'Price': product_prices
})

# Step 5: Convert price to numeric and find the best deal
data['Price'] = data['Price'].replace({'\$': '', ',': ''}, regex=True).astype(float)
best_price = data['Price'].min()

# Output the best price
print(f"Best Price: ${best_price:.2f}")

driver.quit()
```

Explanation of Code:

1. **WebDriver Setup:** We initialize a **Selenium WebDriver** to open the browser and interact with websites.
2. **Navigating Websites:** The `get()` method is used to visit each e-commerce website.
3. **Extracting Prices:** The price is extracted using Selenium's `find_element()` method by targeting the specific class.
4. **Data Storage:** Data is stored in a **pandas** DataFrame for easy manipulation.
5. **Price Comparison:** The script calculates the best price by comparing the extracted prices.

10.3 Project 3: Extracting Job Postings from Multiple Websites

Objective:

This project aggregates job postings from different websites using both static and dynamic scraping techniques.

Tools and Techniques:

- **BeautifulSoup** for static content scraping.
- **Selenium** for dynamic content scraping.

Python Code Example:
python

```python
import requests
from bs4 import BeautifulSoup
from selenium import webdriver
from selenium.webdriver.common.by import By
import pandas as pd

# Static scraping using BeautifulSoup
def scrape_static_job_board(url):
    response = requests.get(url)
    soup = BeautifulSoup(response.text, 'html.parser')

    job_titles = []
    company_names = []
    for job_div in soup.find_all('div', class_='job-listing'):
        job_title = job_div.find('h2').text
        company_name = job_div.find('span', class_='company').text
        job_titles.append(job_title)
        company_names.append(company_name)

    return job_titles, company_names

# Dynamic scraping using Selenium
def scrape_dynamic_job_board(url):
    driver = webdriver.Chrome(executable_path='/path/to/chromedriver')
    driver.get(url)
```

```python
    driver.implicitly_wait(10)

    job_titles = []
    company_names = []
    jobs = driver.find_elements(By.CLASS_NAME, 'job-listing')
    for job in jobs:
        job_title = job.find_element(By.CLASS_NAME, 'job-title').text
        company_name = job.find_element(By.CLASS_NAME, 'company').text
        job_titles.append(job_title)
        company_names.append(company_name)

    driver.quit()
    return job_titles, company_names

# Combine job listings from static and dynamic sources
url_static = 'https://example.com/job-board'
url_dynamic = 'https://example.com/another-job-board'
static_jobs, static_companies = scrape_static_job_board(url_static)
dynamic_jobs, dynamic_companies = scrape_dynamic_job_board(url_dynamic)

# Store the results in a DataFrame
jobs_df = pd.DataFrame({
    'Job Title': static_jobs + dynamic_jobs,
    'Company Name': static_companies + dynamic_companies
})

# Output job listings
print(jobs_df.head())
```

Explanation of Code:

1. **Static Scraping:** We use **BeautifulSoup** to scrape data from static websites where the content is directly available in the HTML.
2. **Dynamic Scraping:** For websites with JavaScript-rendered content, we use **Selenium** to interact with the page and extract job data.
3. **Data Aggregation:** Both static and dynamic sources are combined to create a comprehensive list of job postings.

10.4 Project 4: Social Media Sentiment Analysis with Web Scraping

Objective:

This project scrapes social media data (e.g., Twitter posts) and performs sentiment analysis to gauge public opinion.

Tools and Techniques:

- **BeautifulSoup** for scraping social media data.
- **TextBlob** or other NLP libraries for sentiment analysis.

Python Code Example:
```python
```

```python
import requests
from bs4 import BeautifulSoup
from textblob import TextBlob
import pandas as pd

# Step 1: Scrape social media data (example: scraping Twitter posts)
def scrape_twitter_posts(keyword):
    url = f'https://twitter.com/search?q={keyword}'
    response = requests.get(url)
    soup = BeautifulSoup(response.text, 'html.parser')

    posts = []
    for tweet in soup.find_all('div', class_='tweet'):
        tweet_text = tweet.find('p', class_='tweet-text').text
        posts.append(tweet_text)

    return posts

# Step 2: Sentiment Analysis using TextBlob
def analyze_sentiment(posts):
    sentiments = []
    for post in posts:
        blob = TextBlob(post)
        sentiment = blob.sentiment.polarity
        sentiments.append(sentiment)

    return sentiments

# Step 3: Collect and analyze posts for a given keyword
posts = scrape_twitter_posts('python')
sentiments = analyze_sentiment(posts)

# Step 4: Store the results in a DataFrame
df = pd.DataFrame({
    'Post': posts,
    'Sentiment': sentiments
})

# Step 5: Summarize the results
average_sentiment = df['Sentiment'].mean()
print(f"Average Sentiment: {average_sentiment:.2f}")
```

Explanation of Code:

1. **Scraping Social Media Posts:** The `scrape_twitter_posts()` function fetches Twitter posts based on a keyword.
2. **Sentiment Analysis:** Using **TextBlob**, we perform sentiment analysis on each post to determine the polarity (positive, neutral, or negative).
3. **Data Summary:** The analysis results are stored in a **pandas DataFrame** and an average sentiment score is calculated.

Chapter Summary

In this chapter, you've learned how to implement four practical web scraping and automation projects. Using tools like **BeautifulSoup**, **Selenium**, and **pandas**, you can extract data, perform analysis, and create useful applications. Whether it's scraping market trends, comparing e-commerce prices, aggregating job postings, or performing sentiment analysis on social media data, these projects allow you to apply the concepts learned and gain valuable experience working with real-world data.

Chapter 11: Best Practices and Future Directions

In this chapter, we will discuss best practices for writing efficient and maintainable code for web scraping, explore legal and ethical aspects of scraping, and take a look at emerging trends in web scraping and automation. Python code examples will be provided throughout, illustrating how to implement these best practices. We will also explore future technologies like Artificial Intelligence (AI) that will shape the web scraping field.

11.1 Writing Efficient and Maintainable Code

When working with web scraping, it is crucial to focus on creating clean, efficient, and maintainable code. A well-organized codebase not only helps developers work more effectively but also ensures that projects can be scaled and maintained with minimal effort in the future.

Code Organization

The foundation of efficient web scraping starts with organizing your code. Proper code structure is essential for readability, debugging, and long-term maintenance. Here are some key practices to follow:

1. **Modular Design**: Break down your scraping code into smaller, reusable functions. Each function should have a single responsibility and be easy to test independently. This way, if something goes wrong, you can quickly identify the issue.
2. **Separation of Concerns**: Ensure that different aspects of your project (data fetching, parsing, and processing) are separated into distinct modules or classes. This avoids tight coupling, which can make your code difficult to modify or extend.
3. **Documentation**: Writing clear and concise documentation is a must for every project. Each function should have a docstring explaining what it does, its parameters, and what it returns. Additionally, comments throughout the code should explain the rationale behind specific implementations.

Using Functions and Modules

Web scraping projects can benefit greatly from modular design. By breaking down tasks into functions and using Python modules, you ensure that common tasks can be reused across multiple scraping projects. Here's an example of how this can be done in practice:

Example: Refactoring a Complex Scraper into Modular Functions

```python
import requests
from bs4 import BeautifulSoup
import pandas as pd

# Step 1: Function to fetch page content
def fetch_page(url):
    response = requests.get(url)
    if response.status_code == 200:
        return response.text
    else:
        raise Exception(f"Failed to fetch page: {url}")

# Step 2: Function to parse the HTML content and extract stock data
def parse_stock_data(html):
    soup = BeautifulSoup(html, 'html.parser')
    stock_data = []
    for row in soup.find_all('tr', class_='stock-row'):
        stock_name = row.find('td', class_='stock-name').text
        stock_price = row.find('td', class_='stock-price').text
        stock_data.append({'Name': stock_name, 'Price': stock_price})
    return stock_data

# Step 3: Function to clean and structure the data
def clean_data(data):
    df = pd.DataFrame(data)
    df['Price'] = df['Price'].replace({'\$': '', ',': ''}, regex=True).astype(float)
    return df

# Step 4: Main function to tie everything together
def main(url):
    html = fetch_page(url)
    stock_data = parse_stock_data(html)
    clean_df = clean_data(stock_data)
    print(clean_df)

# Example usage
url = 'https://example.com/stock-data'
main(url)
```

Explanation of the Code

1. **Fetching Page Content**: The `fetch_page` function is responsible for making an HTTP request to the URL and returning the raw HTML content if the request is successful.
2. **Parsing Data**: The `parse_stock_data` function parses the HTML to extract stock data. It looks for each table row (`<tr>`) with the class `stock-row` and extracts the stock name and price.
3. **Data Cleaning**: The `clean_data` function processes the raw data by converting the stock price from a string format to a numeric value.
4. **Main Function**: The `main` function ties all these components together, ensuring the scraping and data cleaning process runs sequentially.

11.2 Staying Within Ethical and Legal Boundaries

While writing efficient code is important, so is adhering to ethical and legal standards in web scraping. Web scraping, if done incorrectly, can violate a website's terms of service (TOS), infringe on copyright laws, or even breach data privacy regulations like GDPR (General Data Protection Regulation).

Legal Implications of Web Scraping

Before scraping a website, it is crucial to understand the legal ramifications. Different websites may have different rules and restrictions regarding scraping. Always follow these guidelines:

1. **TOS Compliance**: Always read the Terms of Service (TOS) of a website. Many websites explicitly prohibit scraping, and ignoring these terms can lead to legal consequences.
2. **Robots.txt**: This file on a website indicates which parts of the site are open to crawlers and scrapers. It's important to respect these guidelines to avoid scraping restricted content.

Ethical Considerations

Ethical scraping goes beyond legality. Here are key ethical considerations:

1. **Server Load**: Frequent requests to a website can overload its server, slowing down or even crashing the site. To be ethical, scrape with care by limiting the frequency of requests.
2. **User Privacy**: Avoid scraping personal data unless you have explicit permission. Scraping personal information like emails or addresses without consent can lead to privacy violations.

Example: Checking Robots.txt

```python
import requests

# Example function to check robots.txt
def check_robots(url):
    robots_url = f"{url}/robots.txt"
    response = requests.get(robots_url)
    if response.status_code == 200:
        print("robots.txt content:\n", response.text)
        if 'Disallow' in response.text:
            print("Be aware of scraping restrictions in robots.txt")
    else:
        print(f"robots.txt not found for {url}")

# Example usage
check_robots('https://example.com')
```

In this example, we check whether the website allows scraping by reviewing the content of the `robots.txt` file. If the file contains `Disallow` rules, we know to avoid scraping those parts of the website.

11.3 Future Trends in Web Scraping and Automation

As web scraping continues to evolve, so do the technologies and techniques that drive it. The future of web scraping is closely tied to advancements in AI, machine learning, and automation. These technologies will enable more intelligent, efficient, and scalable scraping solutions.

AI for Intelligent Data Extraction

AI-powered tools are increasingly being used for data extraction. Unlike traditional scrapers that rely on static HTML structure, AI can automatically recognize and extract relevant data, such as product details or job postings.

Example: Using AI for Intelligent Data Extraction
python

```python
from sklearn.externals import joblib
from bs4 import BeautifulSoup
import requests

# Load a pre-trained AI model for extracting data (conceptual)
model = joblib.load('data_extraction_model.pkl')

# Step 1: Fetch page content
def fetch_page(url):
    response = requests.get(url)
    return response.text

# Step 2: Parse page and apply AI model to extract data
def extract_data_with_ai(page_content):
    soup = BeautifulSoup(page_content, 'html.parser')
    page_text = soup.get_text()

    # Step 3: Use AI model to predict relevant data (e.g., product details)
    extracted_data = model.predict([page_text])  # model's prediction on the page's text
    return extracted_data

# Example usage
url = 'https://example.com/product-page'
page_content = fetch_page(url)
data = extract_data_with_ai(page_content)
print(data)
```

With stricter data privacy regulations, such as GDPR and CCPA, scrapers must ensure compliance with these laws. Web scraping must be done responsibly, and personal identifiable information (PII) should only be collected with explicit consent.

Example: Compliance with Privacy Regulations

```python
def scrape_with_privacy(url):
    response = requests.get(url)
    soup = BeautifulSoup(response.text, 'html.parser')

    # Ensure no PII is collected (e.g., remove personal data fields)
    sensitive_fields = ['email', 'phone', 'address']
    for field in sensitive_fields:
        if field in soup.get_text().lower():
            raise Exception(f"Sensitive data found: {field} - scraping aborted for privacy reasons")

    # Continue with normal scraping logic if no PII is found
    data = extract_relevant_data(soup)
    return data

# Example usage
url = 'https://example.com'
scraped_data = scrape_with_privacy(url)
```

In this example, we implement a function that ensures no personal identifiable information (PII) is collected during scraping. If sensitive data like emails or phone numbers is found, the scraping process is aborted to comply with privacy regulations.

Chapter Summary

This chapter covered essential best practices for writing maintainable web scraping code, including code organization, modular design, and documentation. We also discussed the legal and ethical considerations that must be taken into account when scraping websites. Lastly, we looked at emerging trends in web scraping, including the use of AI and the importance of data privacy compliance. By adopting these best practices and staying up to date with technological advancements, you can ensure your web scraping projects remain efficient, ethical, and compliant with legal standards.

Chapter 12: The Road Ahead: A Vision for the Future

Implementing Tricks and an Example

To use Selenium with Chrome, you need the ChromeDriver executable, which allows Selenium to interact with the Chrome browser. Since you specified the path `"..\driver\chromedriver.exe"`, here's an explanation of what you need to do to set up and use ChromeDriver correctly:

Setting Up ChromeDriver

1. **Download ChromeDriver**:
    - Go to the official ChromeDriver download page.
    - Download the version of ChromeDriver that corresponds to your installed version of Google Chrome. You can check your Chrome version by opening Chrome and navigating to `chrome://settings/help`.

- Extract the `chromedriver.exe` file from the downloaded archive.
2. **Set Up the Driver Path**:
    - You need to provide the path to the `chromedriver.exe` executable in your code. You specified it as `"..\driver\chromedriver.exe"`, which means it is in the `driver` folder one level up from the current directory.
    - Ensure that the `chromedriver.exe` file is placed in the correct directory relative to your script.

Code Explanation

In your code, you initialize the ChromeDriver with this path:

```python
self.driver_path = r"..\driver\chromedriver.exe"
```

This line specifies the location of the `chromedriver.exe` file. It's essential to ensure that the relative path to the driver is correct and points to the location of `chromedriver.exe`.

Then, when you create the WebDriver instance, you provide this path to Selenium:

```python
self.service = Service(executable_path=self.driver_path)
self.driver = webdriver.Chrome(service=self.service, options=self.options)
```

This code does the following:

- `Service(executable_path=self.driver_path)`: Initializes a `Service` object with the path to `chromedriver.exe`.
- `webdriver.Chrome(service=self.service, options=self.options)`: Launches the Chrome browser using the specified `chromedriver.exe`.

Additional Notes

- **Compatibility**: Make sure that the version of `chromedriver.exe` matches the version of Google Chrome installed on your machine. If there's a version mismatch, the driver may fail to open the browser.
- **Path Validation**: If you run into issues with the driver path, you can print the path to verify it's correct:

```python
print(self.driver_path)
```

This will help confirm whether the file is located at `..\driver\chromedriver.exe` relative to your current working directory.

Troubleshooting Common Issues

- **ChromeDriver Version Mismatch**: If the driver doesn't work or throws an error, you may need to update your `chromedriver.exe` to match the version of Chrome installed on your machine.
- **Permission Issues**: Ensure that the `chromedriver.exe` file has the correct permissions to execute. If you're on Windows, you might need to run the script as an administrator.

1. Imports

python

```
from selenium import webdriver
from selenium.webdriver.chrome.service import Service
from selenium.webdriver.common.by import By
import sys
import time
```

- `selenium.webdriver`: Provides functions to automate browsers for web scraping.
- `Service`: Part of `selenium`, used to configure and run the browser service.
- `By`: A locator used to identify elements in the browser by attributes such as `TAG_NAME`, `ID`, `NAME`, etc.
- `sys`: Used to append paths or manage system-level functions.
- `time`: Provides time-related functions, in this case, to pause the program with `sleep()`.

2. Class Definition - `StepstoneScrapper`

python

```
class StepstoneScrapper:
```

Defines a class called `StepstoneScrapper` which will be used to perform the scraping.

3. Constructor `__init__` Method

python

```
def __init__(self,url="https://www.stepstone.de/jobs/data-science?page=",start_pages=1,end_pages=2,driver_path=r"..\driver\chromedriver.exe"):
    self.url= url
    self.start_pages=start_pages
    self.end_pages=end_pages
    self.driver_path=driver_path
    self.driver = None
```

The constructor initializes the class with default values for:

- `url`: The base URL of the website to scrape.
- `start_pages`: The first page to start scraping from.
- `end_pages`: The last page to scrape.
- `driver_path`: Path to the Chrome WebDriver executable used by Selenium.
- `driver`: Initially set to `None`, this will later hold the WebDriver instance.

4. scrap_url Method

```python
def scrap_url(self):
    self.service = Service(executable_path=self.driver_path)
    self.options = webdriver.ChromeOptions()
```

- `self.service`: Creates a service instance with the path to the ChromeDriver.
- `self.options`: Configures Chrome options (though not used further in the code).

```python
des_list_title = []
des_list = []
links = []
```

These lists will hold:

- `des_list_title`: Job titles.
- `des_list`: Descriptions of the jobs (excluding titles).
- `links`: Links to individual job posts.

```python
self.driver = webdriver.Chrome(service=self.service, options=self.options)
self.driver.get(self.url+f"{1}")
```

- Creates a new instance of Chrome WebDriver.
- Opens the first page of job listings using the URL and appending the first page (1).

```python
time.sleep(40)
```

This line pauses the script for 40 seconds, presumably to ensure the page has loaded before the scraper starts interacting with it.

```python
for i in range(self.start_pages, self.end_pages):
    try:
        self.driver.get(self.url+f"{i+1}")
```

This loop iterates over the pages from `start_pages` to `end_pages` (non-inclusive of `end_pages`), opening each page by appending the current page number to the URL.

```python
article_tags = self.driver.find_elements(by=By.TAG_NAME, value="article")
```

- Finds all `<article>` elements on the page. These are presumably job listings.

```python
        for tag in article_tags:
```

Iterates over each `article` element found on the page.

```python
            h2tags = tag.find_elements(by=By.TAG_NAME, value="h2")
            if len(h2tags) > 0:
```

- Finds the `<h2>` tags within each `article`. If found, it proceeds to extract data.

```python
des_list.append(tag.text.replace(h2tags[0].text,''))
links.append(h2tags[0].find_element(by=By.TAG_NAME, value="a").get_attribute("href"))
                des_list_title.append(h2tags[0].text)
```

- `des_list.append()`: Appends the text from the job description (`tag.text`), excluding the job title (by removing the `<h2>` text).
- `links.append()`: Appends the link to the job listing by finding the `<a>` tag inside the `<h2>`.
- `des_list_title.append()`: Appends the job title (`h2tags[0].text`).

```python
        except:
            pass
```

Catches any exceptions (like errors when scraping a page) and moves on to the next iteration.

5. Quit WebDriver

```python
    self.driver.quit()
```

Closes the browser once all pages are scraped.

6. Return Results

```python
    return des_list_title, links, des_list
```

Returns the scraped data: titles, links, and descriptions of the jobs.

7. Main Execution Block

```python
if __name__ == "__main__":
```

```python
sys.path.append(r'.')
scp = StepstoneScrapper()
```

- Ensures the script runs only if executed as the main program.
- Adds the current directory to the system path (though not necessary here).
- Creates an instance of `StepstoneScrapper`.

Summary of the Process:

- The scraper opens a webpage, loads the job listings, and extracts job titles, descriptions, and links from the articles listed.
- The `scrap_url` method automates the process of navigating through multiple pages, collecting data from each one.
- The program is intended to scrape data from a job listing site (`Stepstone`), starting from the first page and stopping at a specified end page.

Possible Improvements:

- **Exception Handling**: The `except` block is very generic. It could be improved to log specific errors for easier debugging.
- **Dynamic Waiting**: Instead of `time.sleep()`, consider using `WebDriverWait` to wait for elements to be loaded, making the scraper more efficient.
- **Closing Driver on Error**: Ensure `driver.quit()` is always called, even if an error occurs, using a `finally` block.

1. Import Statements

python

```python
import numpy as np
import pandas as pd
import scipy as sp
```

- `numpy` (imported as `np`): A powerful library for numerical computing and handling arrays and matrices.
- `pandas` (imported as `pd`): A library used for data manipulation and analysis, especially with tabular data (DataFrames).
- `scipy` (imported as `sp`): A library for scientific and technical computing, including optimization, integration, and statistics.

python

```python
import joblib
```

- `joblib`: Used for serializing (saving) and deserializing (loading) Python objects, especially large objects like machine learning models.

python

```python
import requests
```

- `requests`: A popular library for making HTTP requests, used to interact with APIs and fetch data from websites.

```python
from selenium import webdriver
from selenium.webdriver.common.by import By
```

- `selenium.webdriver`: Used for automating web browsers to interact with web pages and extract data.
- `By`: A utility class in Selenium to locate elements on the web page by various methods such as `TAG_NAME`, `ID`, etc.

```python
import xgboost as xgb
```

- `xgboost`: A highly efficient and scalable library for training machine learning models, particularly gradient boosting machines for classification and regression tasks.

```python
import matplotlib.pyplot as plt
import seaborn as sns
```

- `matplotlib.pyplot`: A plotting library used for creating static, animated, and interactive visualizations.
- `seaborn`: A statistical data visualization library based on `matplotlib` that makes it easier to create attractive plots.

```python
from sklearn import ensemble
```

- `ensemble`: A module from `sklearn` that contains ensemble learning algorithms, such as random forests and gradient boosting.

2. Adding Custom Library Path

```python
import sys
sys.path.append(r'../libraries/')
```

- Adds a custom directory (`../libraries/`) to the Python path, allowing you to import scripts or modules from that location.

3. Importing Custom Scraper

```python
from scrapper import StepstoneScrapper
```

- Imports the `StepstoneScrapper` class from the `scrapper` module (which you presumably created earlier) for scraping job listings.

4. Instantiating the Scraper

```python
```

```python
scp = StepstoneScrapper(url="https://www.stepstone.de/jobs/?page=", start_pages=1, end_pages=100)
```

- Creates an instance of the `StepstoneScrapper` class with the following parameters:
    - `url`: The base URL for the Stepstone job listings, with a placeholder for the page number (`?page=`).
    - `start_pages`: The starting page number (1).
    - `end_pages`: The last page number to scrape (100).

5. Scraping Job Listings
python

```python
list_of_jobs = scp.scrap_url()
```

- Calls the `scrap_url()` method of the `StepstoneScrapper` instance to scrape the job listings. This method returns a list of jobs, where each job includes its title, link, and description.

6. Setting Pandas Display Options
python

```python
pd.set_option('display.max_columns', None)
```

- Sets a Pandas option to display all columns in DataFrames without truncation when printed.

7. Converting Data to DataFrame and Saving to CSV
python

```python
pd.DataFrame(data=np.array(list_of_jobs).T, columns=['title', 'link', 'description']).to_csv(r'../data/jobsx12.csv')
```

- Converts `list_of_jobs` (which is expected to be a list of lists or tuples) into a NumPy array and transposes it (`.T`) so that the data fits the column structure.
- Converts the transposed data into a Pandas DataFrame with three columns: `title`, `link`, and `description`.
- Saves the DataFrame to a CSV file located at `../data/jobsx12.csv`.

Summary of the Process:

1. **Imports**: The script imports libraries for data manipulation, visualization, web scraping, and machine learning.
2. **Web Scraping**: Uses the custom `StepstoneScrapper` class to scrape job listings from the Stepstone website, specifically for data science jobs, starting from page 1 and ending at page 100.
3. **Data Handling**: Converts the scraped job data into a Pandas DataFrame and saves it as a CSV file.

Possible Improvements:

- **Error Handling**: Add error handling for web scraping, especially around network requests or issues with scraping multiple pages.
- **Dynamic Waiting**: As in the previous code, consider using Selenium's `WebDriverWait` to wait for elements to load instead of using `time.sleep()`.
- **Performance**: If the job listing is large, consider handling the data more efficiently using chunking when writing to CSV to avoid memory issues.

Appendices

Appendix A: Common Errors and Debugging Tips

Debugging is an essential skill for any developer. Whether you are a beginner or an experienced professional, understanding common errors and how to troubleshoot them can drastically improve your efficiency and productivity. In this appendix, we'll cover the types of common errors developers face, debugging strategies, and specific techniques to tackle those issues.

1. Syntax Errors

Syntax errors are among the most common issues that developers encounter. These errors occur when there is a mistake in the code that violates the language's grammar rules. They are usually easy to spot because the compiler or interpreter immediately identifies the issue.

Common Causes:

- Missing or extra parentheses, brackets, or braces.
- Incorrectly placed semicolons or commas.
- Misspelled keywords or variable names.
- Improper indentation (for languages that require it, like Python).

Debugging Tips:

- **Use a Linter:** Many IDEs (Integrated Development Environments) come with linters that can automatically point out syntax errors.
- **Check for Unmatched Parentheses/Brackets:** This is a common source of errors. Use your IDE's auto-format or brace-matching feature.
- **Careful with Semicolons:** Make sure that you're placing semicolons where needed, as some languages treat the absence of semicolons as a syntax error.

2. Runtime Errors

These errors occur while the program is running, and they typically happen due to invalid operations or actions that the computer cannot perform. Unlike syntax errors, runtime errors aren't identified until the program starts executing.

Common Causes:

- **Division by zero:** Attempting to divide a number by zero, which is mathematically undefined.
- **Null Pointer Dereference:** Trying to access a property or method on an object or variable that is null.
- **Out-of-Bounds Array Access:** Trying to access an index of an array or list that does not exist.

Debugging Tips:

- **Use Debugging Tools:** Set breakpoints in your code to pause execution at certain points and inspect the values of variables.
- **Check for Null Values:** Ensure that objects or variables are initialized before you attempt to access them.
- **Validate Inputs:** Ensure that user inputs or external data sources are within valid ranges before processing them.

3. Logic Errors

Logic errors occur when the code runs without crashing but produces the wrong result. These errors are the hardest to detect because the program does not crash or raise an error, but the output is incorrect.

Common Causes:

- **Incorrect conditions in loops or if statements.**
- **Misplaced operators (e.g., using + instead of *).**
- **Wrong assumptions about data structures or algorithms.**

Debugging Tips:

- **Print Statements:** Add print or log statements at critical points in your code to track the flow of execution and variable values.
- **Use Unit Testing:** Write unit tests for individual components to ensure they return the expected results.
- **Step through Code:** Use a debugger to step through your code line by line to see where the logic diverges from what you expect.

4. Memory Leaks and Performance Issues

Memory leaks occur when your program allocates memory but fails to release it after it's no longer needed. Over time, this can degrade the performance of your application, causing it to slow down or crash.

Common Causes:

- **Failure to release resources after use** (e.g., open files or network connections).
- **Keeping references to objects that are no longer needed.**

Debugging Tips:

- **Use Profiling Tools:** Tools like Visual Studio's performance profiler or memory leak detectors can help identify where memory is being allocated but not freed.
- **Check Object References:** Make sure to nullify references to objects after they are no longer needed so they can be garbage-collected.
- **Regular Code Reviews:** Regularly review your code to check for places where memory is allocated but not released properly.

5. Concurrency Issues

Concurrency issues arise when multiple threads or processes interact with shared resources in unpredictable ways. These errors can result in data corruption or crashes, and they can be very hard to debug because the error might not appear every time the program runs.

Common Causes:

- **Race Conditions:** Multiple threads attempting to modify the same resource without proper synchronization.
- **Deadlocks:** Two or more threads waiting indefinitely for each other to release resources.

Debugging Tips:

- **Use Locks or Semaphores:** Ensure that only one thread can access a critical section of the code at a time.
- **Thread-Safe Data Structures:** Use thread-safe data structures and libraries that manage synchronization internally.
- **Use Debugging Tools:** Many IDEs have advanced debugging tools that allow you to monitor the behavior of threads and detect deadlocks.

6. External Dependency Issues

Modern software applications rely heavily on external libraries, APIs, and databases. Sometimes, issues arise because of incompatible versions or misconfigurations in these dependencies.

Common Causes:

- **Incorrect API keys or credentials.**
- **Version mismatch between the application and the dependency.**
- **Network or connectivity issues with external services.**

Debugging Tips:

- **Check API Documentation:** Ensure that you're using the correct API versions and have the necessary keys or credentials.
- **Use Dependency Managers:** Tools like npm (for JavaScript) or pip (for Python) can help ensure that dependencies are installed and compatible.
- **Check Network Configuration:** Verify that the network connections to external services are stable and properly configured.

Appendix B: Recommended Resources for Further Learning

Learning is a continuous journey, and there are many resources available for further study. Below are some recommended books, online courses, websites, and communities that will help you enhance your skills in programming, debugging, and software development in general.

1. Books

a) "Clean Code: A Handbook of Agile Software Craftsmanship" by Robert C. Martin This book emphasizes writing clean, maintainable, and readable code. It's full of practical advice for writing software that is easy to understand and extend.

b) "The Pragmatic Programmer: Your Journey to Mastery" by Andrew Hunt and David Thomas A classic book that covers a wide range of programming concepts, from basic principles to advanced techniques for becoming a better software developer.

c) "Design Patterns: Elements of Reusable Object-Oriented Software" by Erich Gamma, Richard Helm, Ralph Johnson, John Vlissides This book dives deep into design patterns, which are proven solutions to common design problems in object-oriented programming. It's a must-read for developers who want to understand reusable solutions.

d) "The Mythical Man-Month" by Frederick P. Brooks A must-read for anyone involved in software development. It discusses the complexities of software project management and the human side of the process.

2. Online Courses and Tutorials

a) Coursera: Software Development Specialization This Coursera specialization covers a wide range of software development topics, including programming, version control, and testing. It's ideal for those who want to deepen their knowledge in a structured way.

b) Udemy: The Complete Developer's Guide Udemy offers a variety of developer courses, many of which are highly rated. The Complete Developer's Guide is a great all-in-one course that covers key concepts such as version control, databases, and full-stack development.

c) Codecademy: Learn JavaScript, Python, or C# Codecademy offers interactive tutorials for learning popular programming languages. Their platform is highly engaging and provides hands-on practice with code challenges.

d) edX: Professional Certificate in Computer Science Harvard's Professional Certificate in Computer Science (CS50) is an excellent way to build foundational knowledge in computer science and software development.

3. Websites for Learning

a) Stack Overflow Stack Overflow is one of the largest online communities for developers. If you encounter an issue, chances are someone else has faced it too. You can search for solutions or post your own questions to get help from the community.

b) GitHub GitHub is a platform for hosting and sharing code. It also has a large community of developers who share open-source projects. Exploring other people's projects on GitHub is a great way to learn from real-world code.

c) HackerRank HackerRank provides coding challenges and competitions to improve your problem-solving skills. It's especially useful for practicing algorithms and data structures.

d) GeeksforGeeks GeeksforGeeks offers tutorials, coding problems, and solutions, which are invaluable for improving your algorithmic thinking and preparing for technical interviews.

4. Communities

a) Reddit (r/Programming and r/learnprogramming) Reddit hosts many programming-related communities where developers can share resources, ask questions, and discuss best practices.

b) Dev.to Dev.to is a community for developers to write and share blog posts, tutorials, and discussions on various topics. It's a great place to stay updated on the latest trends and practices in software development.

c) Slack/Discord Communities Many open-source projects and development communities have Slack or Discord channels. Joining one of these communities is a great way to interact with other developers and learn from each other.

www.ingramcontent.com/pod-product-compliance
Lightning Source LLC
Chambersburg PA
CBHW062226220526
45471CB00009B/3362